T0194965

BOKLIT

INSPIRING, DARING, LIFE CHANGING

Ely Roque Sagansay

WESTBOW
PRESS®
A DIVISION OF THOMAS NELSON
& ZONDERVAN

WestBow Press books may be ordered through
booksellers or by contacting:

WestBow Press
A Division of Thomas Nelson & Zondervan
1663 Liberty Drive
Bloomington, IN 47403
www.westbowpress.com
1 (866) 928-1240

Scripture taken from the King James Version of the Bible.

ISBN: 978-1-9736-8272-1 (sc)
ISBN: 978-1-9736-8271-4 (e)

Print information available on the last page.

WestBow Press rev. date: 1/8/2020

Contents

Dedication

This book is dedicated in memory of my parents (Rizalino 'Rizal' Sagansay and Aida Roque Sagansay). To all my siblings who have gone before us: Reverend Rosendo Roque Sagansay, Reverend Gideon Roque Sagansay, Joram Roque Sagansay, and two other siblings whom their names were not known to us. To my grandmother who made me feel loved – thank you so much.

Foreword

The Apostle Paul wrote in Romans 8:28 that "all things" work together for good. That truth is difficult to believe in the midst of life circumstances that we would never choose for ourselves. Looking back on those same trying times through the lens of grace, enables us to see that God really does have a wonderful plan for our life, with the ultimate goal of drawing souls to Himself for forgiveness and salvation. The hardships this life affords everyone, makes the love of our Savior, Jesus Christ, all the more appealing. When we don't understand His plan in the present, we can trust His heart that was pierced so that we may live. I hope all who read Ely's story will be convinced of that.

I have had the pleasure of supporting Ely in his work in the Philippines and have seen the love he has for the lost. His heartbeat is to see people come to know Jesus Christ as their personal Lord and Savior. Ely's burden for the people of his ethnic heritage is bore out through his missionary endeavors there. Please join me in praying for the people of the Philippines, they are hungry for the Good News of Jesus Christ!

Pastor Tom Downs
Lead Pastor of Gilead Church, Taylor, Michigan
B.S. Baptist Bible College, Springfield, Missouri
M.A. University of Detroit, Detroit, Michigan

BOKLIT
(Book-Lit)

The early days of my life were narrated to me by my eldest brother, Rosendo, with a group of young people during a speaking engagement in Boklit's old church.

"Boklit" is an alyas or (AKA) given to me by our friends and neighbors when I was a little child. But, why Boklit, and what is the meaning of such name or alyas? It was named to me after I had a surgery due to a lump in my neck. I was around 4 years old then. Our parents did not share this story to me- obviously because I and my siblings did not have a good relationship with our father.

The "myth" behind my name was only known to me 26 years after. That was only when pastor Rosendo my oldest brother told me the story back my pastoring days at a small church in Makati, Manila, which my brother was the speaker. Anyways, I was told that that lump became an infection and was so stinky. They actually called that mark on my neck "Biki" [bee-kee] in Ilonggo dialect. When I was a toddler, I was very healthy, cute and good looking according to my oldest brother when he shared the story to us. The neighbors will pick me up, throw me in the air, and catch me, then, let me hold on an iron bar and watched me hanging there for several seconds until I let go of the bar. That was when one of the nerves in my neck got dislocated. The doctors did the surgery on which eventually became the cause of some kind of infection due to the dirty environment I was living in.

1

_.._.

._._

Ely Roque Sagansay

My parents thought that I was already in the process of healing, so they took it lightly in terms of caring of me and paying more attention with my physical problems. Thus, an infection inflamed my neck, which led to a serious physical condition on my life. That was the beginning of my struggles in life without me knowing it as a toddler.

My Story

I was born in a hospital just across the river, a few feet from a tennis court, and in front of a provincial jail. The place where I used to live is called Bacolod City. It was actually named "Baclod" which means "Mound", "Little Hills" or "Hilly". Our village was poverty-stricken, a slum-like area with gangs, gambling lords, violence, and prostitution. In my early years, my father works as a carpenter with a salary of 4.00 pesos a day, which would be about $1.00 during that time. My mother sometimes accepts laundry with about .50 cents a load. Life was difficult for all of us. During those times, my parent's income was not even enough for a decent meal. With eleven in the family, indeed, it was not enough. My siblings and I have to work hard to have money for snacks at school. I have to sell candies and popsicles, shine shoes, and sell newspapers or paper bags to fend for myself. We used to walk about few kilometers to get to school. By the time we get to school, we're tired and drained already because sometimes, we don't have enough in take in the morning. We would eat porridge for lunch and porridge for dinner, and at times, we don't have enough food for everyone during breakfast. On some days, we would eat porridge without anything on it, not even sugar or salt. In a few good times, we would divide a milkfish for the whole family. Yes, the body down the tail will be divided into ten equal parts and the head of the fish will definitely go to my father.

There were times when I will go to school with just plain coffee for breakfast and only to come home in the middle of the day due to an upset stomach. There were times that I could not sleep at night, and it happens for three reasons: first, because of an empty stomach; second, my parents are fighting over money or over my father coming home drunk only to stop when they get tired yelling; and third, due to another gang warfare. Life from my birth was not that comfortable, decent or great as compared to many children in our city and the whole world.

The Unforgettable Spin in My Life

It was the big turning point in my life that really made me think of something bigger than me. The question is- what was that spin? I was about 3 or 4 years old when the consciousness of a Supreme Being came to me in a very unusual time and in a very early stage of my life. How did it happen? One day, I was looking down on the dirt from our bamboo floor, which was about 2 to 3 feet high from the ground.

As a very observant little boy, I was actually looking on the little mound-shaped sand. I was mesmerized by the mound, the ants, and insects that were walking up and down the little mounds until I felt asleep. In my sleep, I dreamed of falling down to a dark and bottomless pit, but when I looked up, there was nothing in the sky; it was totally dark everywhere. I tried to hold on unto something, but there was nothing to hold onto… I yelled and shouted to the top of my voice "Help!" "Help!" but no one came to help me. Then, I started crying so loud for fear, and shouted one more time; "Help! Momma!" I cried so hard out of fear of falling, and no one will save me from such tragedy.

It was when my brother Samson came home from work. When Samson saw me crying, he picked me up and said: "Stop crying now, I have something for you." Samson put his hand inside the small paper bag and showed me the fruit-flavored toothpaste. He opened the toothpaste and squeezed it a bit, swipe his finger on the mouth of the toothpaste, and put a little portion in my mouth. Samson asked me, "How do you like it?" It was then I stopped crying and forgot the nightmare for a little while.

Nevertheless, the unstoppable falling in a very dark bottomless pit leads to my awareness of spirituality. I started to ask some questions right in my fresh mind, "Who is up there…?" Or "What if no one will rescue me from that falling…?" And "What will happen to me if I fall from that dark bottomless empty space?" While I was growing up, that nightmare of falling to an empty, dark, and bottomless pit was still fresh and alive in my mind. Perhaps, it has been God's way of revealing Himself to me. I believe that if God revealed Himself to me in a very early age, He did it to you too in so many ways and so many times in your life. There are some important reasons and purposes why God did that to me and to you, as, well in ways He alone can do. More so, we cannot ignore the truth about His existence and revelations in our lives.

The Kind of Environment I Grew Up In...

Poverty- Believe it or not, poverty was a normal kind of life for me while I was growing up. I see it around the neighborhood, except for a few who has a little bit more than we have had. We have no appliance or home decor except for an antique radio. It was an unusual radio though, of which you have to tap to operate. We live in a house with no power supply, no running water, and no bathroom. We have to fetch water or bathe somewhere else. There was a tennis court made out of clay and shells just next to our house, and we used the opportunity to take a bath while working on with the water sprinkler at the court. I did not know what it means to turned on your *own* shower nor turned on your *own* electric lights not until I was already 18 years old working on a bakery in Manila. I did not know how it feels to sleep on a soft bed until I was enrolled in a seminary few years later. We don't know how to use fork or spoon. When we bring food to school, we wrapped our food with banana leaves.

I climbed the Acacia tree so as not to be laughed at over my lunch whenever there's any. All my childhood, we used fire woods to cook and used tin plates and cups to eat and drink. Back then, that was the only picture of life that I know of. Here in the States, I still use that image to remind myself where I came from and who I was before...

I used my siblings' short pants and shirts because my parents can't afford to buy us new clothes. Imagine, when I ran, I have to hold on onto my pants, or else, I will leave such where I ran from. I never get to wear long pants until I was on the 4th grade when someone gave my mom a pair of striped pants and long sleeves. The black stripes on those pants resemble the prisoner's uniform in our province back in those days. The whole world had no idea how I made everyone from the neighborhood, the people down the road, and my schoolmates laugh their hearts out. I cannot describe the expression on my teachers' faces that day. A few asked me questions such as "How many people have I killed, or if I robbed someone and was in trouble with the law?" Well, for me, it was the best day of my life because I get to wear long pants and long sleeve for the first time, but to everyone, I was that boy who just got out of jail.

I never get to wear rubber shoes until I was in first year high school. I played tennis with just barefoot or flip flops. When I graduated in elementary, my parents has to borrow a black leather shoes, black long pants, and white long sleeves so I could go up the stage to claim my diploma. Again, when I came home from my graduation, I made everyone happy again because I took off my shoes, put them around my neck and walked home with it from school. I was not used to wearing one. I felt like my feet were burning, and I don't know how to walk right and straight. It was a torture for me wearing shoes for the first time. I came home with my black long pants and white long sleeves, but unshod. I laughed to myself when I recalled such experiences and the life that I had at school.

Poverty is the lesser evil I witnessed while growing up in our village. We lived in a very small house, in the small property my parents got from the Philippine government for temporary resettlement after World War II. They actually didn't acquire it for life, it was granted to them after the war. In other words, we were actually squatters. We lived in a 2-bedroom house with an additional bed on the side adjacent to one room. It was for my grandmother. Like I said, we don't have our own bathroom. The floor was made of bamboo, and was set in a dirt floor, and the roof was made of certain palm leaves or thatched nipa, a kind of local palm leaves from a plant that grows in a swamp in that region. It's a thatch made of leaves of the nipa palm that they put side by side on the roof. They call it nipa hut. Our roof has holes everywhere. It leaks when it rains, and you can see the sun when you lay down at day time. We lived close to the airport, and you can see the plane when it's about to land or when it takes off because of the holes in our roof. It's more romantic at night time because it's a see-through for everyone to enjoy the stars and the moon while lying down inside a mosquito net.

Since we have no running water, we like it when it rains; that way, we don't have to fetch water for a week or so. And since we have no electricity, we like it when it's full moon because our house is brighter from the light it refracts. I once thought owning any appliances may require a lot of money for a salary, and that was the reason why our family could not buy one. On my way home from school, I would always passed by the department stores and just look at the televisions, cassette players, long playing records because we don't have anything but an old transistor radio. All of these I never had until I moved to Manila where I worked in the bakery as a teenager.

Gambling- It was a community of everybody-knows-everybody. Even the post office will deliver the mail without an address and with just my father's name on it, but sure enough, they know where it has to go. However, familiarity made gambling rampant, too, and it could be the second lesser evil in the village. Since the whole village knows each other, the people gamble twenty-four-seven without being suppressed. They gamble in various ways such as in tennis, basketball, and ending games— they bet on the endings or the final scores of the basketball competition in television. You name it— cards, mahjong, sweepstakes, sports, etc. But it was one of the things that I did not get into, although I tried all kinds of gambling, I did not really enjoy it. It was a waste of time for me especially if I lost. Unfortunately, gambling in my neighborhood became one of the causes of the fighting, dispute, and violence among young people and their families. I saw my young neighbors and cousins starved because their parents lost in gambling. Thankfully, my parents were not hooked to it as well as my siblings.

Gang Related Violence and Domestic Violence- I know how it feels to be in a neighborhood of gangsters. Even I had my own gang. We hated other gangs from nearby villages, so we always pick fights with them. We will catch them passing by our lane or the main road where we hang out. Then, we will throw stones at them or hit them with a sling shot, or with a weapon called Indian Pana (a metal arrow used with sling shot). If we cornered them somewhere, we beat them up. Now, you may wonder what the local government was doing about it. Well, they may have no time for petty street wars as the whole country was in conflict with the Communist Party of the Philippines and New People's Army. But as for me, these gang-related violence and nonsense killings around the neighborhood did affect my emotional, psychological, and spiritual upbringing.

What I see around is my basis of morals and values. I grew up with so much violence even in our own home. I saw stabbings, killings, shootings, and riots in the jail across the river. It is easy to say that violence was a normal thing to us when I was growing up. Before the then president Ferdinand Marcos declared Martial Law, my uncle who was a broadcaster in a local radio station will always say or report some killings or violence or something that has to do with murders, salvage, and beatings. I was growing up with a desire to kill. My father shaped our lives and taught us to do such thing. He said he would rather see us in jail and visit us there than to see us in a coffin and visit our grave.

My father even suggested that we bring a knife or any deadly weapon for our protection. When I was a little boy, I came home crying because I was bullied by some kids on the street. My dad said to me; "Don't come home crying, you have to fight back. You have to be a tough guy. Kill if you must, but don't be a coward and a sissy." From that time on, I never cried 'like a baby' until the day I met the Lord- when I came to know Him as my Lord and Savior, and when I repented of my sins. For my dad, as I was also told by my siblings, hurting others and killing them if we must is better for us than being beat up, taking advantage of or be killed.

Our dad was the king of violence and domestic violence in our neighborhood. No wonder, I grew up the same, although the good part about me is when I had my own family, I already was a believer. I wonder what kind of life I may have given my children if I did not come to know the Lord. Domestic violence was rampant in our village during those times, and most of it happened in our own home. During those times, domestic violence was not the government priority because of the national problems the country was dealing with. My older brothers had more of the beatings when I was little. Our dad dragged us all to this ugly lifestyle. I always heard him say; "There is no 'Sagansay' that's sissy, coward, and a cry baby". That was the lifestyle that no man in his right mind would embrace. We were forced to do it or we will be in trouble with him if we come home a loser or a cry baby. I heard fighting and families breaking up in my early age until that day that I left the village for Manila which as far as I could remember, I already was about 18 years of age. I saw husbands beating up their wives, and parents beating up their children real hard in public. But nothing is worse than my father.

Violence is a part of life to me and with the kids I grew up with. No wonder, I grew up a violent boy because of gang violence I witnessed in our neighborhood. It was during the time of the then President Ferdinand Marcos' administration when all these nightmares happened. I even saw it within my extended families and distant relatives who were involved in some violence. Some of my father's relatives were killed by either the Communist Party of the Philippines (New People's Army) or by the soldiers or gangsters. So many times we were awakened by the news of hospitalization or death in the family.

Robbery- One of the very few good things I admired about my dad is that despite his vices, he hated robbers. While he worked as a carpenter, he taught us hard work and hard-earned money. When my gang friends lured me to steal, or rob a store, a home or individual, I always resist. I told them, if we ever rob, we have to do it big time. We will enter the military, rob the government with armaments and weapons; after that, we will rob a bank. If we get busted, we will be in the headlines of every newspaper in the Philippines. If we get killed, we will still be in the news papers, but our bodies will be covered by it, too. However, if we make it, then it's time for us to separate and start our own business. While many of those whom I called friends were knocked into the other side of life, of course, that didn't happen to me.

Robbery was something that my neighbors had to watch every day and night. But I am not for it, and I hated it. Robbery is as common and as usual as daily routine in the village. People robbed and steal chickens, dogs, pigs, clothes, and from little to very expensive things and expensive jewelries. Some would even steal fresh fruits and vegetables. The roots of the problems, I believe, were poverty, drugs and gambling.

Prostitution- It was sad, but many of the underage girls I saw in the neighborhood turned out to be a dancer or doing something else in the night clubs at night. It was sad because my hometown was like a little Las Vegas, too. I was a minor when I watched girls about my age dancing naked in the club in our village. Prostitution was one of the things that I witnessed, work with, and been involved in as a teenager. Our house was surrounded by night clubs (A Cabaret) just a few blocks away. Unfortunately, I knew many of the ladies and those who were involved in such wicked business in a very personal way. I would sometimes come and visit some of the night clubs, cabarets, or strip clubs next door or in downtown area, which is just about a mile away. In my early age; drugs, sex, wine, marijuana and cigarettes was not an exploration or testing and tasting moment; it was already a lifestyle for me. I was just 12 years old then.

Drugs and Wine- I was about 9 years old when I first sipped some beers from the left over of the wealthy tennis players near our house. I would just sip out of curiosity, but don't want to get drunk. Every day in our place, there will always be a drinking session, along the street, in the lane, in some houses, or the tennis club. It was impossible not to see a drinking session in the community at every end of the day. My father's no different from them. I smoke marijuana since I was 12 years old, and only quits when I came to know the Lord Jesus Christ in 1982. I also was an alcoholic from that age until I was twenty-two years old. The Lord changed my life instantly. No withdrawal, no struggles or rehabilitation. The only problem I have is I still kept a stick of marijuana and 45 records of some rock music from the night club or disco house that I used to work for. But marijuana, cough syrups, and Ativan and other anti-depressant pills were my favourite stuff. I used to sing in my friend's Folk House where they served beers and wine, and I was just 16 years old. Back then, the Philippines does not have a strong and firm law governing the minors, and the country does not have teeth on its Labor Code and Policies.

Rebellion- It was not my parents fault, and it was not my fault that I was born in poverty and be in a place way different from where I am right now. It was not their fault when they went through a lot of difficult situations in life, actually, almost all their lifetime. It was God's perfect plan for them. It was God's perfect design; it was God's perfect puzzle for us to put together so we could have a message to share. God has a greater purpose, and it is to make others look up to God and be blessed. God wants to accomplish His purpose in my life, and that's the reason why we are here and why we have the ball rolling for God.

I remember it well when someone turned the lights on at night at the tennis court, and I was a ball boy at that time. I would pick up a ball and throw it to the tennis player who will start to serve the ball to his opponent. I was thinking of my life as I was facing so many opponents, and that includes my father, the neighbors and the bullies that I really wanted to kill. The ugly face of my enemy, which is living in poverty for so long as I was growing up as a little boy adds up to my despicable opponents. It was like an endless hard life, and a destiny that I have to go

13

through in life. I remember eating porridge and sitting on a bamboo floor with my siblings because we don't have enough chairs to sit in. My sibling will pick up a can to check if there was salt, and it was empty. The other one will pick up a glass with a label on it that says; "Sugar"— it was empty as well. I was upset and I turned my head towards the door, and slowly walked out to the door and looked around. One of my big brothers Samson asked my mother; "Momma, no more salt?" My other sibling Ephraim asked my mother about sugar; "Momma, no more sugar?" And it becomes annoying, knowing that mother can't do anything about it. And mother will say; "No kids, we're out of everything. Sorry, we have nothing, no money for groceries or even just for sugar." I can feel the disappointment when mother replied with a sad face and desperation. She was hurt from within for not giving something good or the needs of her children. I overheard their conversation, and looked at them from the door where they were standing feeling sad and disappointed as well.

As a little boy, I would open the door of our house and come out in the dark night in our impoverished neighborhood because I was hurting inside, and I would question heaven in the midst of darkness. Every time I would step out of the door of our small house, I will always see groups of men both young and old drinking coconut wine or commonly called 'Lambanog.' I would start thinking to myself, "if they have the money for booze, how come my parents can't afford to buy sugar or salt?" As I passed by their table, I was distracted by the argument and the fighting of the couple next door over money.

I overheard the argument of the couple about money because it was louder than the music that was playing at that time, and louder than the debate of the drunken men just next to where I was standing. I can hear a woman asking her husband, "What did you do with the money, and where is your one week salary?" And all the husband can say was; "Honey, Honey, listen…" And she was mad and yelled at him, "Listen, What!" as she replied angrily. Some of these people don't put their family as their first priority.

As a young boy, this was the common phrase you heard from our neighbors; "You used all your money for wine, for your girls, or in gambling!" I watched one couples trying to tug o war over a few pesos. I may have turned my back and have walked away from them, but the miseries in my lifetime during those days as I lived in a very hostile environment was something I cannot stand on. It was before I came to know the Lord though.

Just a few yards from the drunken men you can step towards the group of young people playing cards and gamble as their parents on the other table were playing mahjong. I walked and watched the boy close to the table where 4 ladies were playing mahjong, and I noticed the boy was talking to his mother at the mahjong table. I heard the boy said, "Mother, can I have .05 cents, I'm so hungry. I wanted to buy some bread for dinner?" I heard the mother said, "Go home and ask your dad or your big sister for food." You can tell of how my small world was so irresponsible by the kind of values the parents in my neighborhood has, and I don't exclude my parents. Remember that my parents were church people in a

Baptist congregation, but I was sure they were not saved. Their fruit can obviously tell as what the Lord says.

> *The Bible says; 16 Ye shall know them by their fruits. Do men gather grapes of thorns, or figs of thistles? 17 Even so every good tree bringeth forth good fruit; but a corrupt tree bringeth forth evil fruit. 18 A good tree cannot bring forth evil fruit, neither can a corrupt tree bring forth good fruit. 19 Every tree that bringeth not forth good fruit is hewn down, and cast into the fire. 20 Wherefore by their fruits ye shall know them. 21 Not every one that saith unto me, Lord, Lord, shall enter into the kingdom of heaven; but he that doeth the will of my Father which is in heaven. 22 Many will say to me in that day, Lord, Lord, have we not prophesied in thy name? and in thy name have cast out devils? and in thy name done many wonderful works? 23 And then will I profess unto them, I never knew you: depart from me, ye that work iniquity. (Matthew 7:16- 20 KJV)*

I observed curiously and looked at the boy's face with some kind of a question in my heart. "Why?" It was because I saw the boy's face dropped with sadness and disappointment. Why people have to go through this? The mother was so mad at the boy and yelled at him for disturbing her on her mahjong moment. His mother shouted at him; "What are you waiting for…? "Look at me!" she said, and yelled again at him; "Go home!" The boy turned his back from the table and started walking home. As the boy was walking home with his face so heavy and my eyes was focused on him, feeling sorry for him. Imagine if you see that every day. Why? Those were the questions I have to battle with.

The boy was looking down to the ground while walking away, and I was behind him following him from a distance. Ahead of us was a huge crowd, and they were very loud. The sad, hungry, and disappointed boy kept on walking towards the crowd while, at the same time, curiously keeps on looking back to me.

I really felt the pain of the people around us who struggled to survive. I can feel that he was afraid of what I may have in mind, and there was fear in me that he may attack or hurt me. We passed by the big funeral gathering. In Philippine culture, they are allowed to hold their funerals along the street, in the house, or open space. It was the wake of my cousin who died of stabbing in a gang war. There was some speculation that he may have been set up by his enemies. As I passed by, I heard the old lady and the cops talking about my cousin and the cause of his death. The mother shared to the cops her heart and her financial condition. It's really hard for everyone there because they don't have money for the expenses such as for the burial. Some people cried over the death of their loved ones, and at the same time, on the expenses, too.

During those times (in the 60's and 70's), insurgencies, the rebellion of the Communist Party, and Muslims in the Southern part of the Philippines really tored down the country. It behooved President Ferdinand E. Marcos to declare Martial Law. I remember I was at the downtown area shining shoes in September of 1972 when it became headlines in every newspaper in the Philippines, and probably in many parts of the world. I was reading this local newspaper about the president declaring Martial Law when I thought of someone by the name of 'Marshal,' who may have a lawyer or may have something to do about the 'Law' was declared by the president as in charge of something. Anyways, when I came home and overheard my parents talking to some of the guys whom I knew may have been in trouble with the law or part of the insurgencies were talking about salvages, arrests, and the military taking control; it was there did I only realized that our land was in trouble. The world around me wanted to kill each other. As for me, I wanted to kill my dad.

I Wanted to Kill My Dad

Our mother was very diligent. She took care of us in the absence of our dad. She would help clean us up and get us ready for bed in preparation for school the next day. That night, my mother did not notice me coming out of our house. She asked my siblings about me, and no one knows my whereabouts. While I was walking on my way back home, I stopped and looked at far with fear. I wanted to hide somewhere, but it was so dark that I could not see the road and the faces of those who walked on my direction. The place was clear, and no one was in the area at that time; but far back, I saw something moving and swaying.

I realized that who was swaying and moving closed to the door of our house was actually my father walking and trying to make it at home because he was so drunk to walk straight.

In our home, everyone was a little busy preparing for bed. I overheard my mother asked; "where is Boklit?" That moment, there was a loud knock on the door. Mother paused for a moment, and walked to the door and asked; "Who is it?" Father replied: "It's me! Open the door, now!" I have to hide for fear to get into the house underneath our 2-feet high floor level from the ground to get inside or else, I will be in trouble. I tried to walk slowly and tried to slip in when my mother opened the door and have father come in first. There were two doors before we can get to our small dining table. Mother noticed me when I came in and pretended she did not see anything behind my dad while I was trying to make my way to the bedroom.

Father greeted mother as he walked in; "Hello my dear?" Father asked with a sarcastic smile and as he looked at mother with his eyes close for being so drunk. "What do we have for dinner?" Mother answered in a very low tone of voice, "porridge." Father repeatedly says, "Porridge? Hmmm, I heard, and I ate that this morning before I went to work, with just sugar, porridge with just sugar, now, now porr, porridge again!" Father stuttered as he answered mother. Mother just looked at me and nodded her head in agreement to what father have just said. She was trying to keep me out of my father's sight. Why? Because if he found out that I am still awake, he will beat me up.

Father walked to the table and sit as he said, "I assumed you mixed it with pork, chicken, or may be fish this time." Mother said with again a very low tone of voice: "No, there's nothing on it. Nothing like that, no salt, no sugar, no… We…" I know it will start a bad-heated argument. Mother paused for a moment and felt so disappointed. She started to show a sad face on father. Sometimes, mother would just walk down to the kitchen with the dishes, and she would place them in a small basin, and cry silently. Then, my dad would start yelling at her, and they will have a fight. If my dad will hear someone outside, he will lure them to a big fight, and he would even come out and bring out his bolo or knife and challenged everyone. He'd do that till midnight.

As tears ran down her cheek, she went back to father with so much anger and held-back emotion. My mom outburst and yelled at father: "And you were out there drinking and smoking! You spent much of your money on wine and cigarettes than what you have spent for your family! You spent more time with your friends and drinking buddies than your family!" She cried louder this time. "You come home yelling at us because you only have porridge without salt, meat and… oh my…!" My father was quiet for a moment. Money was the main problem my parents had to deal with their marriage.

Aida Riza, my only sister, came in to see mother. My sister was devastated to see my mom crying and feeling hopeless. She straightway walked towards mother, tapped her back, and took the dishes from mother. The best thing my sister could do at that time was to be with her and stand by my mom. My dad will also check on my mom if all of us are home already. If one of us is not around, my dad will start to investigate, and question my mother on our whereabouts, what we were doing, and the time we left home and expected time to come home. We always anticipate someone will get hurt when our dad called us to his presence. My dad will yell at us even with just a simple thing like telling us to go to bed already, and that bawl will come with curse and swearing. Cursing us and swearing at us in public is one of his bad attitudes toward us. After dad would tell us to go to bed, we all have to pick up our stuff right away or we will get a spank for disobeying him. I don't see it as disobedience though, maybe just a little delay on his part.

When my father angrily commanded us to study well, he will say it with insult, cursing or swearing. At one time, he even told me that I will not be able to finish college because I was too lazy to study. He told me that he will walk naked going to the downtown area if I finish college. When I finished my seminary time in Manila in 1986, I went back to our province to show my dad what I accomplished, and told him I finished college. I asked him if he was ready to walk naked at the downtown area. He just smiled at me. Of course, I don't expect him to fulfill his promised that day. I know he wanted us to have formal education, but his lack of tactfulness was one of the causes of our friction. He can't say things to us in a very nice way.

We were always careful on how we talked to him because our dad was so strict and a disciplinarian. I don't remember him playing with us or having a casual talk with us. When our dad told us to clean up, we have to clean up or else… When all of us are scattered around the house, and we were told to do something, we have to do such right away, or we will pay the consequences of our slackness. Our dad has a Spanish word for it— "insigida," which means "right away."

I have my own issues, too. I had a bad attitude towards school. Studying and staying in one spot at school for a long time made me bore to death. All I wanted to do from my elementary grade to high school was to be out there working to earn. I would rather work as ball boy at the tennis court, shine shoes, sell newspapers, or be a taxi boy in Bacolod Plaza than staying at school for so many hours, thinking nothing of my future.

A Brief Background of My Family Circle

We live next to the tennis court. Almost all of us became ball boys and tennis trainers and work hard to earn a living. Rosendo, my oldest brother, was a good guitar player, pianist, and musician. Rosendo wanted to be an actor and singer. He loves the songs of Elvis Presley, and tried to imitate his voice, and his style. He tried hard to make a living doing what he loves to do- entertain. Most of us love to read books. For instance, my brother Ephraim loves to write, read his Bible, and set next to our lamp doing these things.

There were times we put our heads together in bed and start talking softly about our father and mother. I was very vocal of my feelings against my father. Some of my siblings were quite with regards to my dad's attitude and way of discipline. I bluntly talked to my siblings about how father was so bad. He was, for me, the worst dad, and too many times, scary. Ephraim would always oppose my idea of my dad with words like, "I don't think so." Yes, he didn't think so because he and my other younger brother, Joram, were very sickly, so they were never scolded nor beaten up like what our dad did to me.

Joram has convulsion, and he was slow learner while Ephraim has heart problem. I would tell them quietly while in bed; "Oh, maybe because you are our dad's favorite or because you are both ailing. You have a heart problem that's why he doesn't scold you. I heard mother told me that; that's the reason why he is not mean to you." Joram would proudly say, "Yes, father is nice to me, too." I would tell Joram in a nice way; "It's because you are so sick, too. You always startle me and wake me up with your seizure. You have some kind of convulsion. Mother said that, and yet, I don't know why you are always crying in the middle of the night."

From my childhood until now, I always had the flash back of my brother's convulsion. I love him so much that when I dislike what he did, and I hurt him, after a while, I had some remorse. At the time, when they took him to the hospital, we overheard my parents arguing about money, about drunkenness, and how father were very harsh to the children, and that, it affects us so much; emotionally, physically, and mentally. We eavesdropped on our parents' heated arguments and hear unpleasant words from my father. It can really make me think that it has something to do with my dad's exercising his authority. There are times we just looked at each other as we listened to the yelling of our parents. I told my siblings and mother: "I don't like father; I hated him so much. I wish I have a different father like our neighbor or the guy in our Sunday school at church or someone else."

Contrary to my two sickly brothers, Samson, our fifth from the eldest, was one of the tough guys in the family. My dad was so proud of him for being tough. Dad actually wanted for him to follow his footsteps; it is to be tough guy, a killer, or someone people would be afraid of. I'm going to share to you Samson's life based on our interview with him and Remigio, my other older brother. The director of Indie film Vic Tiro had the opportunity to talk with Samson and Remigio few years ago. He interviewed them for the movie project that is still on the process.

When my father and mother's arguments and fighting became more intense, it honestly scares and bothers me a lot. I developed an unexplainable hatred to my dad that I don't even want to see his face anymore. If I could turn my back, get away, or hide, so he won't see me, and I don't see him; I would definitely do it. I was the kind of boy who would not care if I see my dad lying in a coffin. I may not laugh but for sure I won't cry. That's the best way of how I can express my hatred and bitterness to my dad. Obviously, I like what I said- I even wanted to kill him.

I saw mom being so mad with my dad, too. Mother was upset with father because of his attitudes towards us, (to me specifically) and Samson. He was being so mean to me. Mother cried because of how he treated his own children, and because of his drunkenness, and his being always furious at everybody. At one time, I heard mother said to him; "Your oldest son left because of what you have done to him and to me. You beat him so hard until he was down. The same way when you were not happy with your other son, you beat him and also Samson". My father will use anything available to beat us if he could.

I started to have some flashback since that time when my father was beating my older brother which became a nightmare to us. I remember I was standing from behind my father when he had beaten up my other brother, and he fell on the ground. He tried to get up, then, he crawled, but father keeps on hitting him like what you may have seen in the movies or television shows. It was then that he began to hate dad and left home, too.

I remember the incident and the place, but I can't remember how old I was. I was startled, scared, confused, and I don't know at that time what to say or do but cry. My brother turned his head back, and he ran to our house. Father did this ugly thing to my older brother outside our house. Picture in your mind: You heard yelling and cursing, after a while, you heard some kind of commotion and fighting, only to find out it was actually a domestic violence. It was about sunrise. I would cease standing next to my relative's house by the riverbank, only then will their commotion stop. It's obvious that my dad don't really care if it was early morning or midnight; when he's angry and wanted to blow up, times and place doesn't matter to him. Mother ran to help him, but she was pushed by father. When father saw he was down, at first, he was kind of budged... but when he saw mother was looking at him and my brother, he started to change his facial reactions like nothing happens.

When I was a boy and mother relate all what my dad did to my siblings before I was born, I can't already believe it. You see, what my dad did to me was just the tip of the iceberg. If my siblings did not leave home and ran away, it could have been worst. All of these happened in broad daylight. If it happens right now in the Philippines, no doubt my dad will end up in jail. I don't know what you would think of a father who castigated his son until he's down, and still continuously hit him. It could be a nightmare for anyone watching the scene. While being calmed down by my sister, my dad just keeps on releasing his anger to appease himself for his evil desire, and to express his anger and ego. If I look back to where my father and mother fought in front of my older brothers, who, at that time, was struggling with pain, I can't think of anything but wish my dad was not born.

I have another flashback of my other brother's fate in the hands of my father when my brother that night was beat up by my father for coming home drunk and really late. If I concentrate and entertain all the evil memories regarding the appalling attitude of my dad, and all the abuses that he did to us, I don't think you will be reading this book today, or having this book in your hand. It was all by the grace of God, and He gave me the grace to forgive and have positive mind set.

When I was growing up watching all these unfold almost every day, I said to myself that I will never do this to my children. I wanted my children to exercise their freedom, and have my love, and most of all the love of God. I can say those because I saw and heard it to many Christians at church. I heard those in our Sunday school class. My other siblings were victims of similar beatings and physical abuses from my father for several times. The trauma in my life just keeps on filing up like an unending paper works in the secretary's desks.

Unfortunately, because of political instability and the problems of crimes and violence, rebellion, and economic downturn in the country; the government did not put so much attention on domestic violence and abuses. Physical, emotional, verbal, and some sexual abuses, I assume, were not the priority of the government during those times, which they did not put some effort to eradicate. If the government at that time had concrete laws on domestic violence, my other cousins should have not been the victims as well.

Had Republic Act 9262, or the Anti-Violence Against Women and Their Children Act come earlier than 2004, I would or may have went to the Mayor's office or Law Firm or Police station or Department of Social Welfare and Development (DSWD Philippines) to report my dad's abusive lifestyle. Yes, it was a lifestyle for him because the night will not end without him looking for a fight, without yelling to one of us, and swearing and cursing, or beating us with belt or stick. Dad will open the day with the same the next morning. Believe it or not, I was always the target of such. The song of Neil Sedaka; "My World is Getting Smaller Every Day" was very popular in the seventies. It was true to me and to my dad because I can see my dad in a coffin one day, and I see myself in the 4 corners of the jail in front of our house. That's how I see his world as oppose to how I see mine.

"DSWD continues to uphold advocacy against domestic violence by Social Marketing | Mar 27, 2018 | News
"As one of the Philippine government's initiatives to address the issue of violence against women, it is urgent that all government agencies take the lead in implementing and enforcing Republic Act No. 9262 or the "Anti-Violence Against Women and Their Children Act of 2004". Under this Act, violence against women is classified as a public crime and penalizes all forms of abuse and violence within the family and intimate relationships, hence all women should be aware where to report cases of violence committed against them."
DSWD Officer-In-Charge Emmanuel A. Leyco said.
Based on the preliminary findings of the 2017 National Demographic and Health Survey (NDHS), "one in four or 26% of ever-married women aged 15-49 has ever experienced physical, sexual or emotional violence by their husband or partner. One in five or 20% of women has ever experienced emotional violence, 14 percent has ever experienced physical violence, and 5 percent has ever experienced sexual violence by their current or most recent husband or partner..." (Google)

Another Reason Why I Really Wanted to Kill My Dad

One night in our house, it was very dark. We have some little lamps with kerosene to keep them going. I was talking to my siblings in a very soft voice and a little reserved. I shared the day my siblings were in trouble. I softly said;

"I remember those days when father beat up Remigio and Samson when they had a fight over food on the table. I saw dad was so enraged, and he beat them with belt, and punched them. Mother tried to stop him, but he was even more mad and wild." As I was sharing this to them, they were so scared to be heard by my father being still awake. But we always hear the commotion and the cursing while we were in bed. Ephraim, my younger brother, was a little spiritual, and he would sometimes say, "Let's pray and sleep. You know, you know, I don't really know what will happen to Samson when he comes home. I bet he will be in trouble when he comes home."

We were all in bed and father was at the table drinking some cheap wine. He will either drink Vino - fermented wine made from certain local vine or a beer. In some nights, he drink 'tuba,' which is a fermented coconut juice. That was the same feeling I felt as that of Ephraim, and the same feelings and statement as my brother Samson have had every time he comes home late. It is- "I don't really know what will happen to me coming home late at night". It went on the whole time I have lived my life as a teenager under my dad's roof.

One night, just a block away from our house in an alley, we had a drinking party with friends and relatives. We were all drunk already, and randomly, I heard Samson said this: "Let's drink and have fun for tomorrow we may die. I don't like my kind of life. I don't like my father; he hated me; I wanted him to be mad at me and really be angry at me. I hate wine, I actually hate drinking, but you know, I'm doing this to make my dad upset at me. That's the only revenge I can do against my dad for his brutality on us." Samson friends don't understand him, so are mine when I tell them how much I wanted to make my father hate me because I hated him so much. Samson has been in a lot of trouble, too, just like me. I heard Samson say this so many times, and I will share to you the detail of his story at the end. "I hated my father and I really wanted for him to get upset and disappointed and be angry with me. He has a very high expectation of me. He wanted me to be like him- a tough guy who would be out there doing bad stuff, committing crimes, and be in jail someday. He wanted me to be like my relatives, and some of my friends who are known for being a tough guy here in our village and the whole province. I fear God, I'm afraid to die, and I don't want to go to jail. I disobey him, and I don't want to listen to him because I wanted to get his attention, because he refused to listen to me."

I was scared of Samson because he gets into my nerves by forcing me to do things against my will, and if I refused, he hit me. But at the same token, I was also worried of his life because I thought he was really rebellious and was making a lot of trouble in our village and city. It's still fresh in my mind that day when Samson came home wounded. I know Samson came home late that night. He had drinking session with friends, and when they became so drunk, they started beating up my brother. My dad was so mad and he suggested to Samson to take with him some weapons next time. My dad told him to have some deadly weapons with him so that in case he gets in trouble, he is prepared. I know that this could sound inappropriate and disgusting to hear; but it was my dad, and it was true.

He did that to me, too, so I was not surprised that day he advised me to be ready to kill and go to prison.

How I Proposed to Kill my Dad

There was no new, good, and high expectation from our father. There was nothing for us we may call 'cool stuff' from dad. I don't remember him bringing something home for the kids, except for new wooden rod or staff to use for his disciplinary actions to those who disobey him. My dad never came home with new clothes, new shoes, or bunch of food and toys for us. All he has for us was a drunk and loud father at night.

It is very obvious already that our life growing up was a cycle of the same circumstances. We live our lives with the same anger, cursing, and yelling every day and night. It was indeed a home of non-stop swearing, and the same time a home filled with hatred and fighting. The most miserable place to live in on earth was our home. It was a wrestling or boxing ring because we always wrestle with the demons, with our dad, and all the evil that was happening inside the house.

One night, dad came home drunk. My mom was waiting for him only to end up the night in disgusts and misery. But it was different that night. We were all sleeping like there was no tomorrow until we were awakened by our parents fighting and heated argument. I got up and peek at the small hole in our wall. Our house had holes everywhere from top to bottom. If I will describe our home or name it, I would call it the wrestling ring with plenty of holes for its spectators to watch us. I heard them yelling at each other. When I checked, I saw my mom trying to pick up her sweater, and she was crying hard. I saw mom stepped out of our house, and she ran out running in disgust, and I can see her disappointment and anger while she was crying. I heard her shouted to my dad; "I am leaving!" To describe their relationship in a very vulgar way, it was terrible and unbelievable for them to be together that long and have eleven children. Even if we have everything inside the house, and millions of dollars scattered on the floor for our disposal (which obviously we don't), I would still prefer to be homeless. I would rather sleep in the park or by the side walk and felt the love, care, and understanding of my father than be with him in a mansion with his abuses.

As mom got out of the house, I ran after her as I was crying and yelling at her; "Mom, come back!" I stopped and cried and shouted louder. I was at the ground kneeling, and then I stood up, and I jumped, and I lied down on the ground, and cried and shout to the top of my voice. I looked at mom's legs like it just kept on going faster and faster. I can still feel the rushed of her feet and the movement of her legs and feet while trying to run away from home and running after my mother. I shouted once more; "Mom please don't leave us!" I cried the more, and I saw mom looked back. This time I plead; "Mom, please I want to come with you. I want to be with you!" Mother stopped, walked towards me and picked my hands up, hold it tight, and then she said; "Come with me" as tears flows down her face.

We walked and walked like it was just an endless walk for mom because she can't figure out, and she did not know where to go and what to do. I asked; "Mom, where are we going?" If I'm not mistaken, it could have been about 2:00 am. Dad's time of coming home would usually be at around 11:00 pm to 1:00 in the morning. We end up in Bacolod Lagoon just in front of Provincial Capitol. I still see the spot where we sat when Director Vic Tiro and I visited the place when we were looking for location for the filming of my story.

In that place while mom was seated and crying, I remember asking mom a very surprising question. I know she did not expect me to ask her that question because I was just in fourth grade. I asked her; "How about if I will just kill dad, so your problem will be finish, and no one will be mean at you, and no one will beat me up?" My mom looked at me in wonder like she was in unbelief. I continued; "My siblings will not be beaten up, too." I took out my weapon and showed it to her.

That very early morning, mom put her arms around me and embraced me tightly, and I can feel her tears touching my face. I felt so much love that early morning. My mother said with so much love; "Son, your dad may be the worst dad in the world, but he is still your dad and you might be his worst son, but you are still his son." She hugged me again and said; "God will not be happy if you do that, you have to fear God". She advised me not to think about it again. She told me the way my oldest brother told me when I was already 22 years old. "Dad loves us so much; he just doesn't know how to express it, and he want to discipline us and protect us, but he doesn't know how to do it the right way". That night, I asked my mom to let me lie down in her lap and asked her to touch my head until I felt asleep.

Do I take this as an opportunity to bombard my father for what he has done to us decades ago? No! That's not my purpose and will never be. As you read this, you might start thinking that I was just trying to find release or catharsis from the misery that I and my siblings went through while we were growing up. You will never see the true color of my life, and my dad's life unless you finish reading this book. You will not see the beauty of this puzzle unless you read, and look from the top until the end of the part of this journey. It is to read, and feel the pain and emotion of what we went through.

From that time on, I was determined to leave home once I turned 18, so I can get away from my dad because it's either I can get killed by his abused or I can blindly kill him. I tried to elope before I turned 18 years old, but it did not work out. I waited until I was 18 years old, so I could leave home. I dreamed to be a night club singer in Japan, and Manila was my stepping stone. That was one of the reasons why I wanted to leave home too. I will talk about it more on the next chapters.

Before I became a teenager and not big enough to fight my dad, when dad has a tiger look especially when he is angry at me, I felt like I was going to melt. I was never scared of so-called monster or witches, but when I looked at dad and he becomes so angry, that was so scary to me. But when I was big enough when I was so angry of him; I felt like I can put him to the ground when my flesh was on the rise, especially I was not a Christian back then. Although I attended church and Sunday school, I don't have the Lord Jesus Christ in my heart. I was just accustomed to be present at church. Also, we were just forced to go to church on Sundays. I can tell that he was beginning to be so weak because he was alcoholic. People in our neighborhood were scared of him too and have a very high respect of him. But when I see him cursing and swearing at any of us, I felt like I really wanted to grab him and put him on the ground. My dad, my mom, my sister, and other siblings will always tell me that I always look like I was angry or wanted to fight back because of the way I looked at him when I was mad. That rage was due to my uncontrolled hate to my dad.

My Childhood and Teenage Life

I love to make money by selling candies when I was a little kid. In some days, I sell popsicles, newspapers, bread, and does shoe shine as my other source of income. I like picking up junk and take them to the junk shop so I could make money when I was with my cousins. I did not want to be dependent to my parents for my daily needs when I was a little boy. I would do anything to make money. I go to the movie theaters, eat at the restaurant, and buy my own stuff from working as a ball boy. I was determined to be independent and be wealthy someday, because I was jealous on some of the children that visited the tennis court to play tennis with their dad, and I observed that they have so much fun and they ate and drink whatever they want. In my mind, I was thinking- 'that's what I wanted to do to my children when I grow up and have my own family.'

How can I forget the churches and Sunday school teachers? There is no way I would and could forget about them. The time, the teachings, and the treasures of love that they (the churches) imparted to me will surely lasts for eternity. I am eternally grateful to Bacolod Baptist Church in Bat-us, Calamba, Bacolod city, and to Maranatha Baptist Church in Home Site. The reasons why I mentioned them, it is because of the impact in my life through their ministry that engraved in my heart by their love and care. I remember every Saturday or Sunday afternoon; someone from these churches will come to our place, and pick us up to teach us the Bible, and feed us with bread or porridge.

The big question in my heart and mind during those times were not from the Bible; but just one big question on why are they doing this to me? We were dirty, stinky, and we were living in a squatter area where no one ever dared to come to put up a business, be it on daylight, and especially at night time. Why would these beautiful and decent ladies and men would hold the hands of a squatter boy, and sometimes carry him and put him in their laps like he was their child?

I cannot forget their Feeding Program. The verses that they made us memorized such as John 3:16 and John 14:1-6 were all fresh in my mind. Believe it or not, those verses are the words I carried with me even when I was drunk or high of drugs or marijuana as I drift away from God and my family. Those verses were used by the Lord to convict me while I was at the night club or while my flesh was enjoying the sins of the world. My sinful acts were many times been blew off by the verses and stories in the Bible that were shared to us on Sunday school extension in our village by the faithful teachers from these churches. What do I mean of 'I carry with me'? I cannot forget what they did to me, even until the writing of this portion of my manuscript. I can't remember their faces, but I remember what they did, their love, and their teachings.

At the same token, I can't also forget the wealthy professional athlete who played tennis at the tennis court in our place. This man was famous during those times, and when I heard he was at the court because I saw him on television, I came close to him to get a nice look at his face, and guest what I got? He said; "Shush, get out of here, you're stinky!"

In 1993, when I was in Los Angeles, California, I was the guest singer and speaker, and he was going to give the testimony about his conversion. I know his family in the Philippines because I get to play tennis with his mom, dad, and his brother. Thus, I listened to him as he shared his life, their wealth and success, his being famous in the Philippines, and his career. He also shared his life after he came to know the Lord as his Savior. After the service, I relate to him about my bad experience with him and how he treated me when I was a little boy. He can't recall, but he humbly apologized. I saw the changed in his life, too, and how the Lord humbled him and used him for God's glory. He became a good witness to family, friends and colleagues.

The reason I mentioned it is that I want you to compare the two kinds of people whom I could never forget in my life. The one was a very successful person and have everything he can offer to a boy like me. The other ones were as poor as me, but they invested in my life with the love that they have for God and people. Their care and the Word of God that they shared to me when I was a young boy made an impact that they don't have any idea how it has blessed me, my family and others. Those Bible students or young people, and Sunday school teachers may have not known the impact that they made in my life, but God knows they did made an impact and God knows who they were. When I was in the night club and disco houses, it was the Bible stories of these Christian friends that God used to convict me and lead me to His cross. It was John 3:16 that they have me memorized that made me look up to God in fear, because of the fear of death and the fear of the second coming of the Lord Jesus Christ. I was so afraid for the Lord Jesus to come because I know I can't be with Him that day.

When I thought things are going well, it was not and never been better. I remember when the Beatles were being so popular that everyone wanted to be like them. Because my dad did not want to spend money for the barber, he was the one who cut my hair. I like it when that old and slow man would cut my hair because I can tell him what kind of hair cut I wanted him to do. For lacked of money to pay for my hair cut, my dad decided to cut my hair. During those times; flat top for old people or military cut, but for the youth and the children, it should be like John Lennon or Paul McCartney or the Beatles. Father imposed his taste of hair cut to his rebellious son, and I'm sure you know what would be the end thereof — war. Yes, it was a war that I could never forget until now. That's the reason I'm sharing this to you.

That moment while my dad was trying hard cutting my hair, I was crying. You know that while you are cutting someone else's hair and he messed up several times because he or she moved a lot and I was very restless, you will surely be upset. I wanted a mirror, so I can see what he was doing, but he did not want me to use the mirror, and it adds up to my disgust. When dad's anger was already filled to the brim, he dropped the scissor and the comb, and he picked me up from the high chair, and put me down on the ground real hard. He was very furious and he was not done yet, he rushed to the corner and picked up the plastic water hose that were already brittle due to its exposure to the heat of the sun, and he beat me up with that hose. I ran around trying to skip the beatings, but he ran after me. Every time he got close and hit me, I see pieces of the brittle hose flying all over me. After he ran out of hose and done hitting me with the hose; I looked at the ground and see the pieces of the hose scattered everywhere around the side of our house. When my mother checked my back, she can't believe what she saw. It was my dad, no one else like him.

I don't know if there is someone else like him, I hope no one else but him. I tried and attempted to commit suicide several times. I tried taking all the vitamin c and the multi- vitamins in our room expecting that I can kill myself with over dosage. I just went nauseas, but nothing happens. I thought of anything possible to end my life. I wanted to be hit by a car and make it look like an accident, but I think the people from Bacolod were not fast drivers.

They drive as meek and as pleasant as their accent. I surely believe God has a greater purpose and plan in my life that's why He did not let it happen.

Unfortunately, that desire became a reality. One school day, I skipped school and went to my friend and asked him if he could let me sell some of his Newspapers. He was the one who distributes the National and Local Newspapers to those who wanted to sell them. It was in a nice and pleasant afternoon when a man across the street was calling me. He yelled "Newsboy!" When I saw him waving his hand and making a gesture on me wanting to buy newspaper, I instantly ran without looking to my left and to my right. I was eager to get to his location and not being pushed out by other newsboys. There was car parked on my left side, and as soon as I ran to cross the street without looking on my left, a car hit me. I did not see the car coming. When I fell, I can see the newspapers flying all over me. I heard people screaming; "The boy got hit by the car!" The newsboy got in an accident!" I heard one of my friend shouted; "Boklit was hit by the car!" and some said; "Take him to the hospital!" The driver took me to the Emergency room.

When I was in the emergency room, I overheard my dad talking and he was looking for the driver. My dad never say; "I love you" to us. He never gave us a hug or gave us a kiss. And he did not show any affection on us in any ways he can. But that day, I was thinking maybe he really loves me. My dad found the driver and the driver apologized to him and paid my dad. I did not get my share but the care of my mom while I was in the hospital.

Adventurous and Overtly Ambitious

When I watched television programs in our next door neighbor peeping in their window, I would pick up an actor, a sportsman, or a singer to copy and be my personal hero. I watched Arthur Ashe or John Newcombe and other popular athletes, and I would say, "I want to be successful and be on Television like him". The same way with the singers I saw and hear like John Denver, Tom Jones, and Matt Monro.

I'm thankful to God because although I was not a Christian at those times, He gave me positive mind set about life and about my future.

I remember my life picking up some junk at the creek that flows from the hospital. I saw a lot of nasty things in that creek that goes through in front of our house unto the ocean. We picked up junk stuff to sell at the junk yard for a few pesos. I did the meanest job to make money as a young boy. But in my mind, I was telling myself- I don't want to live like this when I become an adult, and I don't want my children to experience all these. When I talked to my friends about my desire to accomplished, they were like wondering and some were in disbelief. I told them that I wanted to be a broadcaster, a reporter or a journalist. As a young boy, I already had a lot of dreams to count on. I also wanted to take Statistics, or be a professional tennis player or a singer in Japan. As a little boy, I have so many things going on in my mind.

Some of my friends were happy to be where they were during our young age, but, for me, I really wanted to make it in life. I was even more encouraged when I watched the movie of Walter Navarro (A Filipino actor in the 60's) about the rise of a poor boy from the squatter area and he made it to stardom. He became a popular singer and very wealthy. In my mind, I was thinking, I can be like that. Other than being optimistic, in spite of what I was going through with my dad, I was the joker of the gang and friends, and I was the dreamer.

In today's life, there's so much to be thankful for… But for sure, you can't say that on my time, as a young boy and a young man. Not only that we did not have sometimes food on the table on ordinary days, but on Christmas days or New Year's day. We did not have gifts like what some children have had in many parts of the world. Millions of them just took for granted what they had that others on the other side of the world don't have. We should be thankful we have all the abundance in life on ordinary days and on special days or occasions.

"Thank you" was as hard to say as condolence during my time with my parents. We have no decent bed, not a decent kitchen, and no privacy. Our house was like an open book. I don't have the words to explain it to make the industrialized countries, and developed countries, and the modern world understand what I mean. Nevertheless, some of the third world countries can relate to what I'm talking about, especially to homeless people and people who lives in shanties.

One of the blessing I have was I was making friends with people older than me, and successful people. I became close friend of a millionaire who owned a business and a Folk House where I became his regular singer. I made friends with the lawyers, radio hosts, doctors, and business people as a teenager. I drink and ate with them. Although it was just my connection from my boss and a friend, the good thing is, I was with them in good time at the bar or night clubs like I was their regular friend.

Don't Get Me Wrong!

When I was a young boy, I have high respect for the girls until I had a relationship with the girl not far from where I used to live. She likes me and I liked her, and we started dating. One day, during the Holy Week season, she asked me if I could come with her to the Church. There we went, and I sat next to her. But during those times while at church, all I did was asked her to leave already because I wanted for us to go somewhere. Although we were at the religion that I was not a member, I was respectful to her and her religion, except for the fact that I can't handle the boredom. That girl spent money for me. I don't love her, I just like her.

I met some girls at the night club, in the cabaret, and other places that I was not really serious with them. Those were temporary relationships and it was not pleasing to God. I never thought girl like them- beautiful and in excellent shape bodily will like me. I was skinny, a drug addict, with long hair; I stutter, and very shy person. I realized this when I became older that no matter how beautiful the girl is, and how bad looking the man may be; if they're in love with you; they will give you their all.

Yes, it's either in the name of love or they are just in for the fun of it.

It was fear of being busted and fear of performing on stage that really hunt me aside from the fear that I have from dad when he is angry and I get the beatings. Most of the times, I get drunk to be able to perform whether in the stage or on television. I can't perform without being intimidated, pressured, and being attacked by my shyness. I resort to drugs and liquor to overcome my depressive delusion. If I was not taking something to get me high or intoxicated to get rid of my stage fright, for sure, my performance was a messed.

My Fear of My Dad Did Not Last Long. But the Fear of God was There All the Time

I was afraid of my dad, but that fear did not last long. It was the fear of God that kept me out from doing what I could have done worst in my whole life- kill my dad. All my life as an unbeliever was filled with fear. I miserably dealt with it with drugs, alcohol, and violence trying to get my dad out of my head. Our dad ruled us with fear and not of love and with love. I was also afraid of my own life, and of death. I had fear of God and I know I was very religious, but I did not know the truth. When hate and bitterness developed in my heart; the fear I have of my dad became bygone. I was wondering if my dad had anger management problem, or it was because of his frustrations and desperation, or it could be his trauma on series of traumatic events in his life or lack of education due to what happened on World War II. He only finished fourth grade, but I was amazed to hear dad can speak English very well.

My dad's life was from riches to rags. They lost all their wealth and properties during World War II. My two oldest siblings passed away at a very young age of which their names were not known to us and the cause of their deaths is still a mystery to me. My dad had a dream for Rosendo that did not work out. All these disappointments and tragedies may have contributed to his anger, bitterness and hate. In my personal understanding and analysis when I put together all the information about my father and my grandparents, I have concluded that those were the reasons of his anger problems and a bunch of other issues in life. The traumatic life that he has from his young age up to the time he lost two of my siblings may have dawned on him. I heard a story from my aunt that he (my dad) was really a bad guy when he was a teenager while my grandfather (his dad) was brave, courageous, and intimidating but nice. I assumed he got those from his parents, and I assumed that his upbringing was not with Godly fear.

My life was an open book to everyone in the neighborhood, but in my heart, I kept secrets that no one knows except my mother– 'fear and desire to kill my dad'. As a minor, I know I have the courage to stand and fight back but there was some kind of fear that holds me back. I believe I was the only one who fought back on dad in the later days of my life at home. My youngest brother Gideon a preacher, too, told me when dad was old already that he started to fight back by threatening him. Pastor Gideon shared to me a story about his encounter with dad. He said one day dad was mad at him, and he wanted to hit him. He already pre-planned on what to do the next time dad will hit him, and he did exactly what he wanted to do. He stopped dad and put his (Gideon's face) on dad's face and point his finger on him and said; "You stop hitting me now, and it starts today. If you hit me again, I will put you on the ground. I will punch you! You are an old man, and I can handle you already." From that time on, dad did not yell at him, swear or curse him or beat him up. Gideon left home, too with the same reasons: ran away from dad and find green pasture in Manila. When Gideon was in my church in Subic, he was also in alcohol and drugs. I shared to him the gospel, he came to know the Lord, and the Lord called him to preach. Pastor Gideon took over the church I pastored when I left for the States. He passed away in Dubai due to colon cancer few years after. You see, it was the old lifestyle that caused the cancer.

My Small world in those times was indeed a messed. The world, at that time, was a real mess as I looked at what was going on in our village and the whole Philippines. I was very nosy when I was a little boy. I would sneak in at the corner of our house and listen to my father, uncles, and their friends talking about politics, the Communists, and the killings. I assumed we were in trouble at that time with all the bad news I heard from my parents and older people.

When I was a little boy, I love to iron my clothes although I just had a few. However, while I was preparing the coals and the iron board; I would curiously watch my parents do the Ouija board or spirit of the glass. I watched them do the card readings and hand readings. The practice of horoscope by my old folks and their curiosity on amulets, medium and divination, the used of all kinds of leaves, and other medical alternatives from the voodoos, and necromancy was present at home almost every day. No wonder our home was filled with evil spirits and evil deeds.

I listened to the conversations of the adults. The Philippine culture, the younger generations are not allowed to join the conversations of the adults. That would be considered rude and bad manner. You cannot talk while they are conversing to each other no matter how important you wanted to say. My only way to get informed and satiate my curiosity on the issues was to eavesdrop to their conversation and to be nosy and pretend that I don't hear anything. I was well informed because when I sell newspaper; I would sit in the corner or by the side of the road and read them. I love to read. Thus, I know our world was mayhem. Our family tree and environment in the four corners of our house was a huge messed as well. The evil practices were the reasons why we had the curse in the family.

The messed up and the evil in our home had setbacks. The family that was renting a room next to our house were actually witches. Other cultures may not believe this and agree with what I will say, but in the Philippines, when you say "witch," it more likely means they are after humans. Witches in the Philippines, according to myths, can take a form of a cat, a bird, a wild dog and other animals. Witches in the Philippines are wide awake at night, but asleep on day time. That was our next door neighbor was doing. They also smell fishy. Our neighbor sells fish to cover up their fishy business at night. Our neighbor just across the river was also a witch. You can already tell that our neighborhood is surrounded by evil, and filled with demonic forces. The place was a devil's playground, Satan's workshop, and the demons' stronghold.

When I heard about the news that there was an Ogre in front of our kitchen by the creek and across the house where a witch was living in, my curiosity evoke on me, and I was not afraid to see one. I even got up at 3:00 or 4:00 in the morning to see something out of curiosity. I was not afraid of witches, ogre or something that was evil. I developed this braveness on any evil things because of what my father planted in my heart. Although I was not yet a Christian during those times, my curiosity on those evil forces developed courage in my heart.

I used to be bullied, abused, laughed at, and disrespected, but dad scolded us and beat us if we come home crying or if he had known we're being bullied. He taught us not to be afraid to anybody, and even to kill. He'll be happy to hear he has a child or children who are violent and not afraid to kill or die. This was one of the things that fear on evils did not work on me. Or maybe it was just my curiosity to such things. Few blocks away from our house, my cousin saw a white lady standing on his way as he walked his way home. When I heard about it, I went there at night. I was weird.

I was in California, and I slept in the house church where someone said it was like a haunted house before and, they were curious as to why I was not afraid to sleep there. I sighed. My background will tell why.

It's obvious that I grew up in an environment filled with witchcraft and evil practices. You can feel that awkward and different kind of feelings and spirit in our house. We saw ogre, we saw witch in our roof, and we saw big flying birds outside our kitchen. I believe that we were in need of the Lord Jesus Christ to really free us from those evil things during those days.

> *"Proverbs 5:1 KJV My son, attend unto my wisdom, and bow thine ear to my understanding:" What you've learned from your teachers, professors, and books were understanding or knowledge. What you acquire from God, from His Word, from the preaching and teaching of your pastor is wisdom. What you have learned from Hollywood movies that are filled with sex and violence and immoralities, and so called 'non- traditional family values' are the scope of sin. In "Exodus 35:31 KJV And he hath filled him with the spirit of God, in wisdom, in understanding, and in knowledge, and in all manner of workmanship;" The Bible says; Psalm 111:10 KJV "The fear of the Lord is the beginning of wisdom: a good understanding have all they that do his commandments: his praise endureth for ever. Proverbs 8:11 KJV For wisdom is better than rubies; and all the things that may be desired are not to be compared to it."*

People, Churches, and Organizations that Made an Impact in My Life

I heard so much preaching and Bible teachings growing up in a very "Religious" and so called "Church- Centered Home". When I was 15 years old, I attended the Bible study in our next door neighbor, which I believe was organized by my mother. It was a gentleman from the church who conducted the Bible Study. I actually accepted the Lord during the invitation, but I don't think I was really serious of my decision. Few months after that, I got baptized at Bacolod Baptist Church, again, I don't think I was really serious. In that church, I had a crush, and I believe that was one of the reasons I kept on coming to that church with my three cousins and a friend. Every time we come home, we talked about the girls at church. I actually get bored on Bible studies and Sunday school, as well as the worship service.

I appreciate the effort of Bacolod Baptist Church to reach out to me as a young man. They sponsored me to attend the Youth Camp. They helped me grow in my walk with the Lord, but I think I was very rebellious to God. One day, I even have a fist fight at the church with one of the youth in the choir. But they planted the seed, and it never came void. It has worked in my heart when I was very far from my love ones, especially when I was lost and far away from the Lord Jesus Christ.

My time in the church choir made an impact in my life. As a 15 years old kid, my voice sounded like a girl. I joined the church choir and the music director won't let me sing bass because my voice was terrible. One Saturday night while we were practicing with some of the choir members; I was really restless and loud. In one of the line, I sounded terrible and I know what I did. Our choir director stopped the music and ceased the choir, and looked at me in raged and said; "Ely, you sound terrible, you are messing up, and you don't behave yourself!" She said that with anger in her face. Then, she said this without tactfulness; "Ely, your voice sound like a nail being scratched into a galvanised Iron sheet! You sing softly and pay attention to me, or get out of this choir and go home!" I did, I went home crying, and I did not know what to do. My cousins tried to comfort me and encourage me to go back to church and I did.

But those times when I started coming back to church because I know I needed church, I needed to see the girl I admired, and I enjoy hanging out with the young people. I also like to be with Manong Aaron 'Bebe' who is a singer, and I like to learn from him. He taught me how to play guitar and sing few folk songs. I also did not want to leave church because I have some friends that were older than me. They were all funny guys and they helped me a lot, and gave me some advices. The lady at church who was like a mother or big sister to us whom we called "Manay Pening" or "Phenina" made a big impact in my life. Her love for the Lord, for us, and the work in the ministry was tremendous and valuable. I respect and admire her so much.

All of the people at the church where I used to attend as a teenager were really great people. I love them, and I know they love me in spite of the fact that I was so hard on them and I was a bad boy. The church is very memorable to me. One of the bad memories I have in that church was when I had a fistfight with one of the young people my age, and the other one was older than me. I did not really care if it was at the church or whoever I had a fistfight with. I was an angry boy and hot tempered kid with no purpose in life.

At one time, I interrupted the prayer time because I get annoyed with the other boy my age, may be around 15 or 17 years of age who kept saying; "Yes Lord" "That's right Lord" "Yes, yes…" and other terminologies we used in agreement to the prayers of others. I was so mad that I stopped the prayer time and confronted him and told him to stop his annoying fill in of words while someone is praying. I told him in the midst of the prayer group; "Why do you have to say those words? Why are you annoying and talking and interrupting? Can you just be quiet when someone is praying?" He got mad, and we had a fist fight because I was so mad at him doing such remarks. I know it's funny, and I laughed to myself while writing this portion. It was unbelievable of me.

However, my frequent presence at church during those days was not just about my friends and the fun to be with friends; we also helped the elders in Bible studies, tracks distributions, and visitations. Although I was doing all those good deeds, my heart I know was not right with God. I was living in hypocrisy. I was even sent to a mission field, and joined the evangelistic team in Guimaras Island where I end up in fourth year high school, but I did not get to finish my schooling there because I became a drug addict and a drunkard again and it went from bad to worst. I was the problem, I mean, huge problems to Good Shepherd Fold Academy and to the man in charge we called daddy. I noticed almost everyone in the Orphanage was aloof to daddy, and some of the orphans even told me that they were scared of daddy because he was very strict. Daddy made a big influenced in my life. I remember him taking me to his room, and I thought he would beat me up or scold me for being a bad boy in the Fold. But daddy was way different from my dad by how he talked to me and showed me his love. Daddy shared to me his life from poverty to being the founder and leader of the largest academy, and a huge orphanage in Guimaras Island, Iloilo, Philippines. He shared to me how he started from being a dishwasher and a janitor here in the United States to being the leader and successful servant of God.

I did not put to heart daddy's advice to study hard, and be dedicated to God because of the force and influence of the people around me at that time. I became so bad in the academy and orphanage that they have to send me back home to Bacolod City.

I remember Daddy talked to me in his room about the love of God, God's faithfulness and how he made it in life despite of trials, sufferings, and the struggles that he went through in the United States of America while he was studying as a young man. Indeed God is faithful. It reminds me of the devotional I wrote few years ago. I wanted to share this to give us some good teachings from the Word of God regarding His faithfulness.

In (II Thessalonians 3:3 KJV) it says; "But the Lord is faithful, who shall stablish you, and keep you from evil." God is faithful and He is faithful all the time. It means even in His judgment, we can see the Lord's faithfulness. When we say God is faithful all the time, it means even in our trials and sufferings, in our pain and sorrow, in our joy and extremities and even in sickness and prosperity. When we say God is faithful, it means we refer to its entire creations and what He is doing with it. God cannot change His character as a loving and faithful God. God is faithful even in His Creations- the Natures. (Psalm 119:90) "Thy faithfulness is unto all generations: thou hast established the earth, and it abideth." God's faithfulness is beyond our imaginations and comprehension. There's no word to express His faithfulness to His creations. (Genesis 8:22) "While the earth remaineth, seedtime and harvest, and cold and heat, and summer and winter, and day and night shall not cease." So, what does it tells us Christians? It means that as long as this earth is revolving in its courses with His grace upon it; life will go on and His faithfulness is upon His creations. We can always look back in the past with our eyes focus on God's faithfulness to us. We can always look back to what He has done in the past and give Him the glory for all the things that God has done for you and yours. It's for Him and all because of Him anyways.

> *Whatever God has done for us, He did it and*
> *continues to do it, because of His love for us and*
> *He wants to get the glory in which our Holy*
> *Lord really deserves such. Notice what the great*
> *apostle Paul says in his epistle in (Colossians*
> *1:16- 19) 16- "For by him were all things*
> *created, that are in heaven, and that are in earth,*
> *visible and invisible, whether they be thrones, or*
> *dominions, or principalities, or powers: all things*
> *were created by him, and for him: 17- And he is*
> *before all things, and by him all things consist.*
> *18- And he is the head of the body, the church:*
> *who is the beginning, the firstborn from the dead;*
> *that in all things he might have the preeminence.*
> *19- For it pleased the Father that in him should*
> *all fullness dwell."*

One of my dad's 'Lit that Fire' of anger started from an empty jar. When I got back to the church again, I tried to be faithful and I served God even though I was empty in my heart. I believe I did not take God seriously when I accepted Him in spite of the witnessing, discipleship, and Bible studies. Almost every night that I joined in with religious activities; it seemed to be just a day to day ritual to me. One day, I came home and I did not get to fetch drinking and washing water that day. One of my dad's 'lit that fire' of anger could start from an empty jar. When he comes home and the potted jar is just a little drip of water; war, hate, and swearing and cursing will be overheard for about fifty to a hundred feet away in the neighborhood. Like what happened in the past before I went to the Orphanage to study, I was back to old life and old grudge with my dad.

This time, when I came home and the jars were all empty; it was really different because of what my dad did to me. My dad's anger can trigger in with someone passing by selling something, or to our next door neighbor who are annoying or to something else that he don't like. Every time I come home when I was a teenager from some activity at church, my spirit was high and I was happy. I was enjoying my time walking home from church with my friends and cousin that night. I tried to be the best I could and be a good teenager and a good boy; but my dad's hate, anger, bad attitudes, and his drunkenness and abusive discipline gets in the way.

That day, as soon as I opened the door and stepped in into our home, my father grabbed me on my chest and started swinging me, and dragged me and dodged me. It was scary. Before I knew it, I was looking at him eye ball to eye ball and he started screaming and yelling at me; "Why did you not fill the jar with water before you went to church or go somewhere!" I looked at him in anger. He yelled again; "I don't want you to go to church! Don't you ever look at me like you want to fight back, you understand!" I just nod my head but the truth is, he was right; I want to fight back because I was so sick and tired of him shaming me in public, looking down at me by telling me that I don't amount to anything, and I can't finish school.

I was very sick and tired of him physically, verbally, and emotionally abusing us. My dad made me stand straight, and this time yelled at me and shouted at me and said, "Do you want to fight me!?" He then put his hand hard on me on my solar plexus and I fell back about 6 to 8 feet away from him. You know and I believe you already have an idea of what will happen to a 40 to 60 pounds boy being in the hands of an abusive father, or a 5'8" tall and 150 to 160 pounds adult. It made me think to really do something to get out of my father's presence and abusive treatment.

The last time I felt such pain was when it was about 2 or 3 years earlier. It was around 1973- 1974. It was when an Army officer was very upset at the club because he did not get what he wants from one of the ladies. I did not know that he was very upset, and without any warning, I touched his Army boots because I love it. I said, "You have a nice boots and I like it…" This man was seated at an Army jeep at the passenger side. Before I even get to finish what I have to say, he kicked me really hard. I fell on the ground, and I was crawling, and I can't breathe for pain. I ran for pain and I was afraid he might get harder on me.

Now you may already have a little idea of the pain I felt when my dad hit me. It was so painful that I can't breathe. After that, my dad left without a word, but in my heart just like what I wanted to do to that Army guy who kicked me; I have the desire to eliminate my dad, commit suicide or just run away from home which was the best option for me. Although I attempted to commit suicide since I was in grade school, the inner voice became stronger when I became a teenager. I tried to resort on drugs and wine, and to become more violent, and I blame it all to my father abuses, but it did not help but went worst.

I believe my being violent and not care enough if I die or get hurt was part of my suicidal attitude and mission. I would rather die than live in a home like you never seen before and nothing liked it in my time. What my dad did to me became a stepping stone for me of which I became more convinced and determined to leave home for Manila even though I don't know anyone from there. I also was so determined to have my new life from Manila as my stepping stone to Japan to be an entertainer. The mindset of committing suicide became out of my mind set when I came to know the Lord Jesus Christ.

After that incident, I tried to get some of the information from my cousin who was in the Army because he knew the man, but he refused to give me the information. He was one of my targeted individuals at that time that were on my list to kill after I joined the military. My plan was to organize a team, and steal some firearms and ammunition with a sole purpose of killing all the people who were mean to me, and the next goal was to rob a bank.

The Beginning of My Dream

I know I will come to the point where I will be separated from my parents and pursue my dreams and ambitions in life. Leaving Bacolod City and be away from my parents is the only way for me to be able to go to Manila and pursue my dream of going to Japan. This was just the beginning of fulfilling such dream.

What I did after that nightmare with my dad. I started to hide little by little my clothes so I can run away from home without their knowledge. I was in fourth year high school at the time when I planned my stowed away from home. I went to 3 high schools for fourth year (12 grade) 3 times and did not finish it. I had too many absences in the class although I passed the exams and tests. During those times, I had a girlfriend who just graduated from high school.

When I was studying in Night School, I sang in one of the event at school. My teacher heard that I sing in Folk Houses and on the radio and television, so she asked me to sing in some of our school shows. I did not know that I had an admirer at school during those high school days. One day as I was walking in the school gym, I was greeted by people who heard me sing. It was after my television appearance that I started to get invitations to perform. I was invited to school's graduation, in parties, churches, and radio programs to sing. One day, the school program coordinator invited me to sing in their school function. It was in this event that I was fully known to my secret admirer, which later became my girlfriend. I was on the stage singing, and a beautiful girl was on the side staring at me, and it caught my attention. The girl was with her friend and I can discern that she really like me.

On the side of the gym, she and her friends had a conversation. I turned my face towards them while I was singing, and began to desire to know her. I did not know she also wanted to know me, and talked to me. During those times, I was so arrogant and I felt like I was the new star at school. During my performance, I can sense that she was interested in me, so I approached her and get to know her after the show. Our friendship turned into an intimate relationship. I even asked her to marry me, but things began to changed when it was known to everybody including her relatives.

I will talk more about what happened in the next chapters. I remember when I came down from the stage and walk down to where they were, the first thing she said was; "I love your voice." I did not know that she already told her friend which was also my friend that she really hope she could meet me and get to talk to me one on one. Her friend said; "I will take care of it, he is on 4th year at Night School too". She was very surprised when she heard that I was in fourth year high school at 'Night School', and had been to 5 High Schools and could not even finish it. My friend said; "He is not dumb or flunked on any subjects, he hated school, and had so many absences." My friend did a good job on covering, although she was right.

When this girl said to me; "Hello, how, how are you? How's, how's your friend?" I know it was not just the performance at the stage that she had in her heart but me. I stuttered when I talked while growing up, may be because of the trauma that I've went through from a very young age until I was a teen ager. When she asked me those questions, I stuttered, and I don't know what to say. I never had a girlfriend or dated a girl *seriously* because I don't feel like the girls would be interested in me. A drug addict, an alcoholic, and a boy who is living in a poverty stricken environment. She stuttered because she may have been scared to be rejected, but I stuttered due to my trauma from my dad.

One day, at school during our break, we see each other at the place we called Rendezvous. She started asking me personal questions. When she asked me, I have to ask her again because of the noise at school and the distractions. I asked; "What did you say?" She repeated the questions more clearly. We began to talked and chatted a little bit until we became more comfortable to each other. As I talked to her, I closed my notes and looked at her again, and I can't control myself and I compulsively said to her; "Wow! You're so beautiful… you are… you're so, so pretty. If I only knew that the one talking to me was this beautiful; I, would, would not… seriously, I won't let them distract me as I pointed to the friends and classmates who were teasing me. And, and I would not, re-really care about my, my notes anyways."

During those times, I was busy studying for an examination at school. This time, I shake her hand and I seemed not to let it go. She nicely asked, "Are you done shaking my hand? Do you want to let go of my hand?" I said; "Oh, I'm so, sorry, I… I…" Before I finished talking, she said, "It's okay… Uhmm, it's really nice to meet you too." I responded to her in a very nervous manner and soft voice; I said, "Nice to meet you, too…"

When we both about to separate ways, I turned my back to leave, but then I courageously went back to set up a date with her. Eventually, after we were introduced to each other, she confessed to me that she was actually waiting for me to propose or set a date with her. I assumed

I know what many of my readers would be thinking- it sounds like a script or looks like a Hollywood scene. You may think that this sounded like a script; yes it's like a script but it really happened. It was because Filipinas here are generally conservative and they were not as aggressive as some of those who grew up in big cities such as Metro Manila.

This time I bravely proposed that we see each other again. I asked her for a date, and if she wanted to go somewhere to eat or drink. Fortunately, she would like to go to the movie instead. Thus, that week, I had my first date, and with a girl to be with and to sit with in the movie theater. We watched the movie of the 'Abba Concert.'

I was thinking of taking her to our house, but I was so ashamed to bring her there, so I brought her to my aunt's house instead which is nicer and a big house, too. I lied because I don't want to lose her, but I think she get to figure it out that it was not our home. We talked about our favorite music, artists, singers, sports, and family. The corny part was having a theme song, favorite color, and other things that sounded weird these days. It was my opportunity to open the invitation for another date, but this time we agreed to meet in a restaurant, and then, watch a movie. We meet several times after that meeting at the school's quadrangle. We shop together, we eat, and sometimes she will be with me in my performance in some of the functions. My girlfriend was from a rich family; thus, she always pays for our dates, but when I do have some, I spend for her, too.

One day, when she came home, she was informed by her parents that her uncle wanted her to study college in

Manila and at the same time, work for him. In one of our dates when we were in a park, and then went to seashore, I noticed that she was very quiet, and she seemed to have some serious problems. I curiously asked, "What's wrong? You have been so quiet and sad; are you sick? Are you alright?" She replied, "I'm not sick and I'm alright." I kissed her but still she was very down, and I thought she was going to dump me, and she just don't know how to say it, or where to start. Again, I asked, "What's the problem then?" My girlfriend started crying and shared to me her parents' planned for her. I believe her parents heard and knew about our relationship. She cried and said; "My parents wanted me to move to Manila to work and finish my college there. I believe they know about you and that we have been seeing each other."

She told me that they found out that I was dating her, and that was the reason why they send her to her uncle in Manila. When my girlfriend told me this, I was devastated. I wanted to marry her right away. She said, "They want to keep me away from you. They know what kind of person you are. They know you smoke, you drink, you do…" I interrupted her, and I stood up from the sea shore where we were seated in the sand near Bacolod Plaza. "I will come with you. I, I mean, I will, I will follow you wherever you would be in, in Manila. My girl responded in desperation; "How? You don't know anyone in Manila, you don't know the place, and you don't have a job there." I firmly told her; "I will be there with you as, as soon as you get there and, and you know, as soon as possible. I met a doctor and he, he became my good friend. We played tennis together… and, and he comes to our night club to drink and listen to me sing. He drinks with my boss at the club, so… I can ask my, my doctor friend if, if I could come with him, and help me find a job in, in Manila, or at least help me find your place."

My girlfriend was very concern about my plans. She did not know I have so much in my mind that I desperately wanted to go to Manila. In her curiosity, she asked me; "What kind of job?" I tried to convince her that I was willing to be with her. I was willing to marry her before she would leave for Manila, so I won't lose her. I told her, as always I stutter; "I can work in a tennis court as a, a tennis trainer, in a night club, as a dishwasher to, to start with… or any job, job, that, that could help me get some kind of access to, to the business owner, so, so I could pursue my dreams. In, and in the fu-future, I can audition to be full time entertainer here and or, or in Japan. I can sing in one of the block at, at least one or two nights a week… and, and save some money. We can get married as soon as possible."

I can't believe she was really willing to ride on. She gave me the assurance when she said; "It's up to you. I trust you, and I love you so much. I know you will not leave me." I felt the ease and peace in my heart when I heard her say those words. I said; "I, I won't, I love you, and I never been so, so in love… I will not leave you." Of course never been so in love because she was my first love. It was not a puppy love or something tantamount to an infatuation. We hugged and we kissed, I hold her hands and made a vow to her. I assured her I was serious with what I said. I promised her I said, "Sweetheart, once I'm in, in Manila and, and have a job as a singer in a club; I,

I will pursue my dreams of becoming an entertainer in, in Japan, and I, I'll come back for, for you and marry you." She hugged me again and she was crying really hard. I tried to comfort her by scratching her head and tapping her back, but to no avail.

We were both preparing and packing our luggage and bags for our trip to Manila. She flew ahead of me to Manila. I ride the ship with my doctor friend because the doctor had so much stuff to bring in to Manila. That night in our house, while I was secretly packing my stuff, I was distracted by the black briefcase of my brother who is a pastor in Baguio City. I came closed, I touched the briefcase, and I had a flashback of the Indian preacher at the Bacolod plaza. I was reminded again of the message on the brief case of an Indian preacher- "Jesus is Coming Soon, Be Ready!" I had a flashback of the Indian preacher picking up the black briefcase and lift it up as high as he could, and show everyone the sticker as he preached the gospel.

I remembered some of the people and children were mocking him even some of the foreigners. The Indian preached; "God sent His only Son, He died on the cross for your sins, He was buried and rose again the third day. He is coming back according to the Holy Bible. He wants you to accept Him as your Savior and Lord. He wants you to believe in Him and ask Him for the forgiveness of your sins." But I ignored these messages as I thought they're all in the mind, and they don't really matter. All the messages from the church preaching, in Sunday school, and its extension near our house, and the messages of the Indian preacher did not really matter to me.

I imagine that day and time where my girlfriend would be travelling in a bus, or in a taxi and be at the airport, got off from the taxi; she hugged her parents, say goodbye and went in to the door of the airport. She stopped and looked back and wave goodbye again, and I could feel like she was saying goodbye to me, too.

My Hide, Then, Seek

I and my friend were playing tennis; my friend notices that I was not very serious and don't play well at that time. I hit the ball and my friend was curious why I seemed to have a bad attitude at the court. My friend asked me what's wrong with me… "You're not serious, you're like, I don't know. Are you alright?" I said; "Yea, I'm alright." He was angry, he yelled at me; "No you're not! You seem to have a very different attitude at the court today." I walked to the back court and stood there for a while at the same time I was looking far and curiously staring to this guy who was coming. I noticed him walking toward the tennis court. I got annoyed of how he dressed up and by the way he walked. I had a 'bad trip'. That was the (lingo of the youths) during those times.

Out of my arrogance, I walked toward this guy. He stopped in front of the court and watched us play. While he was standing there, I stopped playing and walked right in front of this guy. My friend on the other side of the court asked; "Why? What's wrong?" I did not really pay attention to my friend; instead I just kept on looking at this tall and muscled guy. As I got close to him I already have a plan. Then I asked my friend for a 'time out' and to excuse me. My friend said; "Time out and hold on it is…"

As I stood in front of this guy, I angrily confronted him and yelled at him. "Hey! Wait!" He asked nicely; "What? Are you talking to me?" I said; "Yes!" and I swear. My friend was standing there and he did not know what's going on. As I walked towards him and approached him and get closer to him, and I arrogantly said to him; "Wait! Hey! I don't like the way you walked and talked and your school uniform is very formal. I laughed sarcastically. That was the start of trouble and misunderstanding which leads me into a position of endangering the lives of others and putting my family in nightmares and shame. I was arrogant, violent, and did not really care of others, and I was so selfish and jealous of others. It all leads to my bad judgment and unacceptable decisions in life as a teenager. In my life as a teenager, I broke the law, hurt other people, and paid for its consequences which are to hide, remorse, fear, and shame to my love ones.

During my teenage days when I went through problems with my love life, with my father, and as well as with myself- I wish I did not do what I did to other people who were innocent and were just doing their things. But just like what we see out there with those who were blinded, people that are in drugs and gangs; the remorse, and the unbearable fear, bad conscience and the conviction are all too late. Once the law is after you, there's nothing that you can do but hide. I made a mistake, but before it was too late, we were reconciled and iron out our differences.

I remember my brother telling me recently about the nightmare I left my parents after that wicked deed that I did.

There are nice people and good children whose parents were educated, decent; never smoke, or drink or does drugs and don't hang out with bad kids like me but they became a victim. Some youth are very nice and smart but they became victims of some young people who were blinded and lost. On my part, I was just a jerk at that time. My bad decisions were because of my frustrations to my dad being so abusive, and my girlfriend who was leaving me for Manila. But it should not justify my evil deeds and it has consequences.

It reminds me of the writings of Apostle Paul in the book of Galatians, it says; "[7] Be not deceived; God is not mocked: for whatsoever a man soweth, that shall he also reap. [8] For he that soweth to his flesh shall of the flesh reap corruption; but he that soweth to the Spirit shall of the Spirit reap life everlasting. [9] And let us not be weary in well doing: for in due season we shall reap, if we faint not. [10] As we have therefore opportunity, let us do good unto all men, especially unto them who are of the household of faith." (Galatians 6:7- 10 KJV)

I was really astounded when my mother and younger brother wrote me a letter, and telling me that an enemy of mine would want to see me in Manila. I was very suspicious, and I thought he is coming for me, and execute his revenge on me in Manila. It would be easier for him to hide from the law if he had killed me. It's funny how I organized some of my friends telling them exactly what to do if he would do something stupid on me. I asked them to watch me and my signal, and watch him (my enemy) as well. I asked them to watch my back so that I'd stop him if he hit or harm me. The book of Proverbs says, "The wicked flee when no man pursueth; but the righteous are bold as a lion." (Proverbs 28:1 KJV) It was really true in my life when I was not a believer yet. I always felt like I am being pursued by my own shadow, by the law, and by my own enemies. People who have good intentions, I looked at them as enemies. Friends who were good and nice, and wanted to do the right thing, I looked at them as enemies. Why? Because that's what the Bible says. It was my reactions even to good and right actions of other people, and even in their good intentions. I felt like I am being pursued by my own shadow.

Even those who looked at me during those times were considered my enemies already. I thought they were staring at me because they were in pursuit of destruction and trouble, and that I perceived them as my enemies and distracters already. To me, a single stare is considered a threat.

My Brothers Told Me This…

One night, while my family was having dinner, there was a loud knock on the door of my parents' home. There was soft music playing on the radio and some brief news. I was told that the Policemen in the neighborhood from the police station were standing by the door of our house. When my parents opened the door and they were greeted with "Hello, we are from the City Police Station Criminal Investigation Department, and we are looking for 'Alias Boklit'. We have a search warrant from the provincial judge, and we want to have him surrender in our office or we will definitely arrest him and file charges that could be more serious." Mother looked at everyone on the table. My siblings and everyone on the table and on the bamboo floor stopped eating and just watched my mother talking to the authorities in awe. While the cops and my mother were standing in the dirt ground inside our house around 2 steps up to our bamboo floor, everyone in the house were all silent trying to capture the conversation about me and my case. There was a total silence as they listened to their conversation. Mother said, "I'm sorry, I don't know where he is. I was just informed by a boy about the incident, and he never came home since yesterday."

I have an uncle who was a Radio host and a very well known broadcaster in our place during those times. His name is Rudy Paclibar, he passed away a long time ago. I was told by my younger brother that he heard on the radio the news about me and the incidents. There were other incidents and violence and other problems I caused in our village, but this one was way more serious that it was in the media for couple of days. My brother narrated to me what he heard on the radio.

My uncle reported; "We have Breaking News! It is bad news because the boy that was involved, the boy that the Law Enforcers are looking for right now is my nephew. He is involved in serious physical injury, and he left the victims on the ground. Boklit, this is your uncle

Paclibar, and if you hear me right now, please call me or surrender through me at the radio station and I will be here waiting for you. Son, I will promise you, nothing will happen to you and they will not harm you. I will help you with whatever you need. Just surrender peacefully and you will be fine."

I was into hiding from the law, and no one knows that I already bought a ticket going to Manila. Back then, buying a fare for the ship to any part of the country is just like buying a bag of chips at the liquor stores. Some people would just hopped in on the ship to go anywhere in the Philippine archipelago. Samson should be the one who really be on my shoes because he was the one whom my father tried to groom to be his successor as the tough and violent guy in our city and probably the whole province of Negros Occidental.

I really don't have any idea what it feels to be searched by the cops especially if it involves my entire house. I wouldn't know how my parents and siblings must have felt when the cops looked for me inside that stilt nipa house. After checking every room and every corner of the house, the cops may have stopped their search and talked to my parents of my surrender. My parents were told by the Police: "Well sir and ma'am, if your son Boklit showed up anytime, please don't let him go and please call us right away. We will leave you our number, and just like what we said; he will not be hurt." My father said; "I will make sure to turn him in, and yes we will do exactly as you said." The Police just said; "Thank you for your trust."

While we were in my hotel room last 2016 in Bacolod when my brother Ephraim was sharing this to me; I recalled of my life when I was a teenager, and how I've hurt people and my parents as well. I believe I made my love ones in trouble that day. The first Sagansay who was wanted of the Law was an eighteen years old boy who was disturbed, distressed, discouraged, and depressed because of what was going on in his life.

I Was Hiding My Identity, but to No Avail

One day, I came home very early in the morning. I tried to hide my identity by wearing a cap, and tried to cover my face with a piece of cloth, but it was to no avail. I tried not to be identified by the neighbors. Unfortunately, I did not know that my father was at the door waiting for me to come home, I thought he was at work already. My father was drinking coffee and smoking expecting for me to come home anytime soon. When I tried forcefully to open the door of our house, I was surprised to see my dad lightly open it and my father clapped his hands as he sarcastically welcome me home. My father congratulated me and said; "Congratulations! You made a name on television, you are famous. You are very well known to the cops, too. You made it in the Folk House and now on the radio, but in a bad way."

Back in those days, folk songs was very popular. Some of the popular artists that I love singing their songs were 'John Denver' 'Peter, Paul, and Mary' 'America' and others who made a name in Folk Songs. Folk Houses was everywhere in Bacolod City on the 70's. It was then when I tried to make a name in music business as a teenager. I started as a 15 years old kid singing at the church choir. I, then, tried to sing in birthdays, Christmas parties, Graduations, and other special events. I tried televisions and radio, and be the guest singer in hotels and restaurants that provides musical entertainment with the intention to make it big someday. My dad was not happy with me in spite of my accomplishments as a kid. When I stood there in front of him, all that I did for myself and the name I tried to make were just a piece of trash to him. He was so mad at me that he did something I can't forget in my whole life time although I already have forgiven him. He confronted me. Father, then, hit me on my tummy, mugged and hurt me several times. He dragged me and pushed me to the wall and yell at me; and took his belt off and started beating me up.

He yelled at me very early in the morning: "You came home bringing with you this shame on our name, bringing with you this sick thing. Shame and police record... You came home a wanted kid because of what you have done...! You're a traitor! You're a traitor because you said you want to have a fair square with him, but you tricked him, and then you ran away!"

While he was yelling at me and released his anger on me on what I did to the boy, I was thinking, I thought this is exactly what he wanted for us to do? I said; "It was a fist fight, I, I challenged him, and he- he agreed. I just used my brain to put him down." Father: "Your brain!" Father hit me again really hard. This time, I was down and in severe pain. I crawled and tried to get up, but I can't for pain. He said; "You go to church and at the same time you are causing problems in the whole community and city. You put our family in shame and disgust. You don't do your responsibilities and duties here at home. You are always out there until midnight! You made me sick! You go to church on Sundays, yet skip school, smoke marijuana, drink wine and smoke, and now, violence!" My dad did not know that I had been involved in gang war. During those times, sling shot and Indian Pana (arrow) were our weapons.

My dad was furious, and he was restless; he did not know what to do with me after all the bad physical contacts. This time, I have the guts to talk back and fight back on him because I already have planned pinned down. It was the plan to escape. I mumbled; "You, too. You go to church on Sundays, but you, you're a drunk after church… You swear, you curse and you are abusive." Father shouted; "stop mumbling!" He asked me "What did you say?!" I looked at my father and said; "That's what you want, that, that was exactly what you wanted me to do, right? You, you want me to rather hurt people than, than to be hurt by people. I (I cough) – you rather wanted us to kill and be in jail, than be hurt or killed. You say that to my siblings in front of me, and I hear, I heard you say that to them several times. You would rather visit us in jail than in cemetery or hospital." He angrily shouted to the top of his voice; "Stop!"

Father slowly walked to the window, took a deep breath, and turned his face on me; he instantly grabbed me in my chest, pushed me, and come after me, and his hand was hard on me. I was in pain again. I crawled again, but he tried to lift up my head as he yelled at me; "You are hard headed and rebellious! You have no future and can't finish school!" This time, I fought back because I know I will be gone in few days. "I got it from you! I hate you and I wish, I, I was not born in this family. This home is, is like jail for me!" I cried and point my finger to my father and said, "You are like the evil forces in my life!" Father was more outraged this time. Father tried to grab the wooden bar but was stopped by mom. My siblings can't do anything but cry and just look at each other in fear. When mother let loose of me to stop father; I, then, took the opportunity to run away. I went to my aunt's house and made a phone call to my girlfriend. We talked for a while, confirmed the plan and then, hang up.

It Made Me Think of My Miserable Life

I remember that day when he hit me with the plastic brittle hose when I was nine or ten years old. You are reading this, and you might think it was unbelievable of him doing that to a very young boy. I wish we had cell phones during those times so someone could video tape such cruelty and post it on social media or call 911 and report the abused. Mom's common statement at home was "That's enough! Please, I will take care of that for him, please, have mercy." It's always fresh on my mind every time our dad hit us. My mom would always be there to pacify dad's anger, abuse, and rage. She was always there standing between us.

I intentionally come home late, and as usual I get in trouble with my dad. It was because I have no choice but to stay long and late at the tennis court club house waiting for the customers to go home so that we can collect our money as ball boys and consume or take home their left over. I take home some of the food and dad would really be mad at me. The pride of my dad, his anger, his hate and ego clashed at times with mine, and it's all because of the depravation, hunger and poverty that we were into. Yes, I felt like we were depraved of food and other good things in life that we were willing to steal if we could or beg and fight for little things such as leftover foods and drinks. I would sometimes come home with packed of leftover food, and father would really be angry and burst out like we committed something unacceptable to the whole world. He would really be mad like a hungry cow.

He did not want us to live like beggars, but our lives were almost as the same as the homeless and beggars. We were living in a stilt Nipa house with countless holes over our roof, with bad dilapidated, half-timbered walls, no bathroom, and with just bamboo floors. I remember the time my dad told me that if people are sick, then, we will definitely be get sick too due to contamination or if their sickness are contagious such us tuberculoses or hepatitis. It was because we drink the left over beers and soft drinks of wealthy customers at the tennis club. We also eat the food from the same plates and spoons of those who would leave their food on the table after their meals. My dad had a good point when he tried to stop and scared us from consuming their left over. Our lives were so miserable that we were so envious of those who had enough or are wealthy. We did not care about sickness or contamination; we were starving, and we need food- good food that is.

I think of those days when I was at the tennis court having a debate with some of the wealthy, smart but atheist customers made me more conscious of God and spirituality; but at the same time a drunkard, smoker, and drug addict. Yes, as a young boy, I talked to these people about God, and it made me wonder how in the world these highly intellectual persons with nice cars, good paying job or great business don't believe in God? I would look at myself, and I start thinking- here I am as a young boy struggling to make a peso, so I could have money the next day for school. The tennis court club house was both a place of refuge for me and a place of sin. I've seen, and I've done or worked with others in committing some of the abominable things in the sight of God that I cannot even say or write in seclusion. Nevertheless, it was also the place where I learned hard work. I had hard earned money, and I learned the hard way as I grew up in that environment.

The place where I first had my first taste of how it feels to be yelled at by an American right on my face while his hands were on my neck and hit my head on the big metal of chicken wire. It was because I was very loud and I was trying to annoy this man. I got what I deserved at that time. I was already told to stop annoying him, and I did not stop. I think I was having fun speaking English words with him that I tried to distract him while he was playing by shouting; Ball coming! Time out! Hey Joe! It's Coming Joe! I was thinking may be the Americans were really different from Filipinos. The Filipinos can handle those things, but this American man was furious, and he can't handle the annoying kid like me.

In one occasion, I was the ball boy of a Chinese wealthy guy. I insulted this man about the bread he bought for us to eat. I believe I told him he was cheap. In his anger and rage, he bought a bag of bread and threw them on the ground and stepped on it and said to me; "My life will not be affected and my money if I will do this!" He was so mad that my cousin has to take me out in front of him. I was so silly that in many instances; the players would chase me with their tennis rackets because I intentionally made them mad, or I did something stupid. It was still clear to me that day when one of the old men in the court really hit me hard with his tennis racket that I was running and hiding underneath the tables and chairs in fear and pain. At a young age, I wanted to kill that man though he will be next to my father, at least. I even wanted to vandalize his beautiful new car but was advised by my friends not to do so. To add to this, I swore and cursed at some customers and tennis club members. It was almost nothing and seemingly a flippant thing for me to stupidly make people mad and angry of me. I had the attitude of being annoying when I was a young and arrogant boy. I love annoying people, but I hated it when people annoyed me.

I Led the Strike

I remember it when the members of the tennis club were so demanding but they were lax in giving us an increase as ball boys and tennis trainers. I was one of the leaders who were making some troubles as we did our little strike at the tennis club. We organized our own strike. We did not report for work. At night, we throw away stones, garbage and human dirt at the tennis courts as expression of our dislike to the new president of the tennis club. Some of the kids my age also hated him that they even wanted to vandalize his vehicle while some of them vandalized the tennis court with me in the middle of the night.

We were all mad at the arrogance of the new president, and I really hated the oligarch during those times. In my hate and anger, I tried to motivate some of my friends to join me in messing up the (Clay and Shell) tennis courts. We made some potholes and messed up the whole place with broken bottles, junk, and other unwanted stuff. I did not even know what I was fighting for at the time except for money, and my hate for the man. I was not fighting for others or for their rights or the abuses of the wealthy, but for my benefits and hate. I know I was not going to win, but I did it anyway.

The next morning everybody at the tennis court was disheartened to see what we did. Sure enough, everybody was pointing to me and my cousin. We were in big trouble with the wealthy because of what we did to the tennis courts. Fortunately, there were people and tennis club members that were nice and understanding that they even negotiated with us and asked us to stop the so called Labor Strike of ours. We were back to work after a few days. It was worth the fight because they increased the fees for ball boys and the hourly fees for the tennis trainers.

My Life as a Young Boy was Filled with Ups and Downs Already

My life at the tennis court since I was 7 years of age was filled with ups and down until I was eighteen. I was living a life of misery and uncertainty already. I know many of my readers and followers on social media may have the same question as you have while reading this. "How…?" "Why…?" I have definitely some answers to such questions, of which also I can share all the hates and violence I have with other children my age and those who were older than me. I was so envious of other children for what they have in life. I was envious of their good parents, their things, their wealth, and the cars their parents drove. I felt like life's wealth was not fairly distributed and were only given to those who deserved it.

When I think of the abuses, the hate, the bullies, the poverty and every pain I was going through as a very young boy, the only way out and to end it all was suicide. I remember coming home from the tennis court discouraged, frustrated, and felt hated that all I can do best was to go straight to our kitchen and I picked up a kitchen knife, and attempted to commit suicide. Was I suicidal? I believe so. When I was a young, poverty-stricken boy without the feeling of love from father and siblings, life, then, was meaningless and useless. The only thing that stopped me from doing it was because I was so scared too of so many things, specifically death. I think that was a blessing in disguised for me. I tried overdosing myself with the multivitamins my parents acquired for free from the Community Health Center; but I did not succeed, and I praise God now that it did not happen.

It was really hard to comprehend and accept such kind of life if not for the Lord's grace and mercy. I blamed others for the hardships I had as a young boy. I blamed my dad for the kind of life I had while growing up until it came to my mind when I said to myself- I tried to always remember and put this personal principle in my life while growing up as a teenager. 'When I grow up, or become an adult and married, I will never do this to my children. I will never let them go through this hardship, and I wanted to have a happy and full of love family tree. I did, and I can say, I made it in life by God's grace.

I never heard my dad say to me I love you or write me those words even when I already was a teenager working in Manila. I don't remember him treasured my birthdays and celebrated it or something. If you are in this kind of environment, it's so easy to get adapted to hate, violence, and even in hunger and poverty. You will feel like it's already a part of you. My dad's attitude and dealings with me was unacceptable to anybody, but due to what I was going through with him, I began to just accept it blindly until I came to realize that it was not right.

You have to accept it whether you like it or not. That's what I felt when I was in that kind of life and environment. Even when I was just jesting and hurting someone due to my disturbing attitude, to me, it was just a part of fun and a part of me. I even love it more if people will laugh at it.

I remember a boy my age grabbed the chair, and before he put his back on it, I took off the chair. You already know what happened to the poor boy. He fell on his back to the ground. But one thing you did not know that it was a ground full of small pea like stones, hard and dirty ground. I can play over and over of my life if it's a music, but I will be very ashamed of myself if this part of my life where I've hurt a lot people, and put others in danger is played even in private settings. If it be played, it must be with a purpose and must be God honouring. I'm sharing this to give everyone a good picture of how evil and disgusting attitude I had when I was a teenager without the Lord in my heart.

There are a lot more of related bad attitude that I have had as a lost young boy, but to exposed the details of sin and disgusting things I did which are very inappropriate is not acceptable, but to make it known as sin in general I believe is understandable. The tennis club was supposed to be the place for health consciousness, family time, and sports; but it was a place of sin, disgrace, hate and immorality. It was there where I learned all kinds of sin. I witnessed and learned smoking, drinking, weeds, prostitution, swearing, observed homosexuality, and learned gambling at the tennis club. These are just some of the detestable acts. The rest of my life that I can't say it anymore, write it or put emphasis on it because it was so wicked? It was so wicked that I am so ashamed of myself every time I think of it. It's always be there in our sub- conscious although it's been cleanse and washed by the blood of the Lamb and been forgiven by the Lord Jesus Christ. You will never imagine.

I was the most bullied boy in our village while growing up; until one day, I was coming home crying only to be beat up and scolded, which led me to be more brave, tough, and hateful to people. When I was a boy until I became a teenager, I get used to my dad yelling at us around the tennis club. I got used to his Spanish termed of cursing and swearing, and his use of racial slur or words, of which I only realized it was racial slur when I became a Christian. There was not a day in the tennis court club and in the village that do not have drinking sessions, gambling, violence, or fist fighting. Hate became a part of me because of the motivation and influenced I adapted from my dad. The bad influenced of our dad to us to be hateful of people, and as when we were at the point of not to care for others even if you hurt them or even kill them. He taught us the principle that no one in the Sagansay family must be bullied by anyone. What happened to my older brother was one of the awful events in my life as a teenager. It was when my brother came home bleeding. He got in trouble with some of the guys, which leads to unnecessary fighting. My dad, as usual, was unhappy.

Begging for Food

I was a beggar for food. Many times at night, we would wait for the people who were eating in a restaurant to get done, and when they're done eating, we would go after their leftover of foods, and drinks. It was only if it was in an open restaurant like we see in the open market or at the Mall where there are some fast food restaurants and food they sell just right at the bar. In a decent family restaurant, we befriended the waiters or the chef, so we could ask them to bring us the leftovers. Sometimes, they would ask for money, but we don't mind giving them money for good food. One day, as I was seated by the side of the restaurant, while I was waiting for my friend and cousins, I desired and enviously be like them in those tables filled with food. I was there to just watch the people who were eating at the restaurant while I was starving. I can only wish. I walked back and forth by the kitchen and by the door. I did that to actually check on the customers' left over. I checked with the chef, and waiters if they were ready to hand me over the leftovers if there's any available already. I can't resist the hunger. I, therefore, asked the chef, only to be scolded and got a snap on the back of my head.

Then, I came closer to the chef and said; "Hey boss" I plead. "Can, can I have some leftovers, a, a, I'm starving." I stutter because my nervous breakdown kicked in when he gave me a big hit on my head. Although I was so mad, but because I was hungry, I ignored the chef's rudeness.

The chef asked me; "You hungry and poor kiddo, get out of here and you stand by there and wait!" He was mad because we became an eye sore to the customers. I walked away very sad and was disappointed that I walked out kicking an empty can… then I heard a voice calling… when I looked back, it was the chef calling me. The chef was shouting; "Hey! Hey kiddo, I have something for you, I just got your order!" The chef had a brown paper bag in his hand. It was a bag of leftovers. I grabbed it and started running. The chef called me again. "Hey, you forgot something!" he yelled. Then he made a gesture of "Where's my tips?" I reached out to my pocket and get a peseta (.20 cents in paper Philippine money during those times) and offered it to the chef. He looked at the money, and I looked at the food. He paused and he was hesitant to accept the money, but I was thinking differently. He thought peseta was not enough, and Mr. chef was doubtful of the offer and actually refused although he did not say anything about it. I tried to grab some more coins… and chef said; "Forget about it."

It was about that time that while I was enjoying the dinner that my friends arrived. As the custom of our land, we always offer whatever we're eating every time someone showed up; be it at home, at work, or in public. I asked; "Do you want some?" My friends says; "Sure" "Yes, we're hungry, too." "Thanks Boklit". I said; "Not all of it, I wanted to bring some for my family." I and my friends started to enjoy the dinner together, and they talked about how their days were doing. Everyone was happy about how they made money, how they ripped off people, and some begged for money.

We talked about our plans and our dreams. I looked at myself and compare the rich people around us. Looking the difference in our clothes, their nice cars, and the food they eat. Then, I broke the happy conversations with my remarks and said; "I hate my life, I, I hate my, the family I belong with, and, and I, I hate my kind of living." They all stopped eating and looked at me in wonder. I can tell because of their facial reactions. They started asking me questions. "What do you mean?" "Are you alright?" I reluctantly answered; "Yea, I'm alright." After we ate our dinner, we went our way home.

He's My Father

I walked home from downtown (Bacolod Market) so nervous and worried what I may go through again when I come home and dad is home already and drunk. All my friends know that my father was very strict and disciplinarian. They all know that I will be in trouble when I get home. As we passed by the night clubs near the provincial jail along Gatuslao and Burgos Streets my stomach started to crumble already for fear of what I may have from the hands of my dad. They (Potot, Bukaw, Mait, Popoy, Mari) not their real name all asked if I was alright. I said; "No, no I'm not, not all, alright. It's so hard and painful for me to watch our father being abusive to our mother and us. I want my father to stop, and... and end this hurtful attitude." One of them asked me if I consider suicide. Like I said,

I tried to attempt, but by God's grace, it did not happen. Sometimes, I think, I really, really think about it, but I don't know how. My friends just looked at me in silence. I bowed my head down, looked up, took a deep breath, and just kept quiet, which also makes everyone quiet, too.

One of my friend picked up the stick and started hitting the ground and the stone with a small stick and said; "Why did your father hit you all with hard wooden staff? I don't get it?" I remember the story shared to me by my older brother Samson about my mom and dad having a fight while having dinner. I don't remember the pieces of the things involved and the start of it. But, I remember it was dinner time, and I remember my dad coming home with a wooden big stick. He was excited and my mom curiously asked; "What's for the happy face and a big smile?" My dad excitedly answered back; "No more belt for the kids, because I have this…" My mom was so furious. Who won't get mad, anyway? Mom and dad had another fight while we were having dinner that evening. My dad hanged the stick on the wall and told us that he will use it if we rebel or mess up.

I Attempted to Commit Suicide, Again…

One Sunday morning, I came home with so much hate in my heart. I just hated what was going on in my life in terms of my relationship with my dad, the people who tried to bully me and all those who looked down on us because we were very poor. I went home and went straight to the kitchen and contemplating of ending my life because of my hate to so many people and my bad circumstances at home and at the tennis court. I will talk more about the detail on the next chapter.

At one time, I attempted to commit suicide again with different means but I'm grateful to God He did not let it happen. It was stupid thinking and speculating on my part. Therefore, suicide will not work for me. Obviously you may have notice I mentioned so much about suicide because as a teenager, it was the only thing I know as a way out because I can't leave home.

Remember suicide is not the answer to any problems in life. Ending our lives will not help instead it will become a problem to those who will be left behind. It will be a great pain and sorrow that our love ones will shoulder if we end this life by our means and in our hands.

If I jump from the top of the building, I don't know either if it was a good idea. When I talked to my friends about suicide, all they could say were; "Why would you want to die?" "Suicide is stupid." "Remember, our Sunday school teacher said, "Do not kill." Suicide means you are killing yourself. My friends would remind me that it's bad. They have no idea of the pain that I was going through. I told them 'it's because life is so, so hard for us; we are very, very poor, and dad is violent. People looked down on us. My father and my mother always fight. My father will always curse, and swear on us. Who would not want to commit suicide if you're in this kind of home, and with this kind of father?'

My dad has a different and opposite mind set and principles in life than many others. If you're bringing leftovers because no one can afford to buy it, I believe bringing it at home is not a bad idea. That was just my idea as a young boy. My dad's anger boils down to the brink of killing us if he could when we bring in some food from the tennis club or somewhere else. He is suspicious that these leftovers contain some kinds of bad bacteria or contagious virus from sick people who touched it. Moreover, he was dubious that the person who touched it has tuberculosis or hepatitis. But these differences in principles were not the cause of hate and anger.

I developed hate and anger not only in my personal life, but to my dad and others. I tried to finished up my life because of my hate to those who I wanted to beat up because they said something to me that I don't like, or because they are messing up with me. I don't want to be teased, or be made fun of. Sometimes, I would come home depressed because I hated people, I hated myself, and I hated my dad. One Sunday morning at the tennis court, when my cousin intentionally hit me with the tennis ball for no reason, I was so mad, and I went home to get a kitchen knife because I wanted to stab him to death. I end up just holding the knife and placed it on my wrist while my heart trying to feel if it hurts. Whatever happened to me outside of our house, my mind will always go back to our home and the misery I have with my father.

As his common practice and day-to-day routine, father comes home late at night and is always drunk. He knocked on the door and my mother will get up from bed and lighted the lamp with the match that was on the table. She then would go to the door and opened the door for my dad. My father will walk straight to the table and sit. My mother will go to the kitchen and prepare the food for my father. While mother was busy preparing father's dinner, my dad would grab the cup to get some drinking water. The war will start from there... If it was just a drop of water on it, he will check the other jar, and if it was empty, the match of the night will start. My father will be outraged and will start yelling and swearing.

Often times, my mother will try to balance the situation and tell him to tone down his voice because its midnight already. Unfortunately, dad will become more outraged and tell her that he doesn't care about the neighbors even if he woke them up. He will then continue shouting and say that if they have the guts to come and fistfight with him, they can come out anytime and ask for it.

My father will then start smashing the plates and cups on the floor. He was furious and devastated. My dad will always do that and always check on our jar. The two jars are where we stored our water. The one was a (Banga) an antique earthen jar which we used for drinking water, and the other one is (Tadjao) an old antique water container of which we used for washing the dishes and hands. He will always asked questions such as "where have you been?" or "You know that school is done, and it is too late to come home for a young boy like you?" and he would always ask why there is no drinking water in the jar, and no water to wash his hands or the dishes in our really big antique jar we called 'Tadjao'. Even though we answer the right answer or the wrong one, we will be in trouble anyway.

Thus, it does not matter anymore because we will suffer the same consequences.

The Hope I Learned from Sunday School Classes

If you come home every day feeling like there is a monster waiting for you at the door or by the table, you feel what I felt. But God is our hope to any problem whether big or small, bad or worst, resolvable or not, God alone, and He alone is our help and our only hope. The Bible says; *"12 Teaching us that, denying ungodliness and worldly lusts, we should live soberly, righteously, and godly, in this present world; 13 Looking for that blessed hope, and the glorious appearing of the great God and our Saviour Jesus Christ; 14 Who gave himself for us, that he might redeem us from all iniquity, and purify unto himself a peculiar people, zealous of good works. (Titus 2:12- 14 KJV)* It means that our hope is not in man, in money or material things in life, it's not in our good circumstances; but in God through our Lord Jesus Christ. It is in the free gift of salvation that brings us to eternal life in heaven. It is also in the Lord Jesus Christ's second coming.

The nightmare happened again when I came home from selling newspapers after school, and then went with my friends to the restaurant to get some leftover food.

On our way home, father was on the alley going to our house, and I was stopped by my father, and he yelled at me. I was scared and startled, so I nervously covered my face and said, "What!" You know what it means when your children answer you like that. I was arrogant in my answer. I was disrespectful of him and I was trying to hide my anger of him. I felt embarrassed in front of my buddies being yelled at in public. I felt like telling my dad 'shut up!' and 'go home!' On the other hand, if you are a son or a daughter, you know what I mean if you have such attitude. My dad took a deep breath and shouted, "What!" I addressed him "Tatay" means "Father". I said; "Tatay I, I got some food for, for you all…" I know I will never win over him so I offered him food, and I was thinking the food I brought in might pacify his anger of me. My dad was so furious at me anyways, and he scolded me and swore on me right at the alley.

We were few feet away from home. He came close to me with a tiger look and started yelling at me louder; "Yes, leftover foods!" Father took the food, grabbed me on my chest and dragged me towards our jar. Father grabbed my hair and made me look at the inside of the jar and said, "Watch!" This kind of scenario happens almost every week. I know we were at fault, but sometimes the consummation of the water can't be controlled by anyone especially if everyone is at home. It was the cycle in our home that made us all walked through the days and nights with nightmare.

My dad will swear at us or beat us all when he comes home without water in the jars or we did not wash the dishes. Even though we did not intentionally missed fetching water or wash the dishes, his hands will still be heavy on us. I remember, one day, I was coming from the tennis court and I was tired from working as a ball boy.

My dad called me and took me to the earthen jars and let me watched while he was pretending to get some drinking water, then my dad dodged me while he was getting some water, and... he sarcastically said, "Ooooops." While he was looking at me with an angry face, I felt like I wanted to run for fear of him. As my mother observed us she can tell that I was nervous and very scared of what father might do to me, and father was indeed very angry at me, as always. I did not look at him at the time while he was talking, and it made him angrier. He made me stood up straight, and he looked at me right in my eyes and shouted really hard, "So you went to school, sell newspapers, worked at the tennis court doing ball boy job; and you never think of your responsibility, and took care of our home, our drinking water, and even for wash. We have nothing! You heard me, nothing! If our house is on fire, there is nothing to stop the fire, nothing!"

My father walked to the wall and took the new stick, and he slowly walked towards me while he rubbed it, and you got the picture. I was sweating, shaking and softly crying. Father yelled at me really, really loud; "Why? Why you did not fetch some drinking water today!" Mother was disgusted and disappointed of my father's scandalous attitude. I don't know if my dad had double standard at home in his discipline to us. My dad was very nice to my one and only sister Aidariza and some of my siblings especially with Remigio. He was very strict to me and his eyes and outraged were always on me and he gave me a hard time. He was also nice to some people especially if he is not drunk. I wondered if he was double-faced (as I call it back then). My mother reacted, and started gathering all the dishes left on the table, yelling while explaining to my dad, but dad did not care.

I remember how the fighting and yelling from my side to my mother's side quickly ensued. Mother shouted at him; "Your son was at school, and he worked after that, and he already told you!" Dad responded with a louder voice; "Shut up! I'm not talking to you!" Mother ceased from what she was doing and tried to explain to my father everything. I remember mother was telling her friends she has nervous breakdown, and I can tell when she talked to dad; she was shaking. I saw mom talked to dad with her lips shaking and mumbling. "I, I was supposed to fetch some water... but..." Dad interrupted her; "No you're not... it's not your responsibility to fetch water! It's his responsibility, and his siblings' duty, and not your job to do that!" You can tell that dad was really after me. It's true, his eyes were always on me, and how he can get to me. If you are thinking of favoritism in the family- I was never a favorite. Its way, way opposite and everyone knows it at home and the neighborhood, and probably the whole community.

Father turned his anger to my mother, then he sat down and with a tiger looked in his eyes on me, and he began to be quiet. Imagine when you thought it was over; then he put his face closed to my face, and slammed the table really hard. He yelled at me to the top of his voice; "I don't want you to come home with that jar empty, do you hear me!? I want you to fill it up every day, do you understand!?" I was scared, and some of our neighbors were already in bed, but some were just listening in their homes as my father carelessly confronted me. His rants in the middle of the night were so demeaning. I was ashamed of myself to our next door neighbors knowing that in some houses there were some of the most beautiful girls in the neighborhood.

Despite my father's routine, the neighbors won't just mind. They won't report him to the cops. The cops will not care with such 'minor' problems in the community. If there was Social Media back then, I could have been the daily viral and famous persona for being verbally and physically abused by a drunkard father. I will probably be on television as a material for daily news updates on abuse and fund raising to help the needy and beat up child.

He yelled at me as he grabbed my old shirt, which choked me. I just nod my head, crying under control because I did not want to be hurt again. I said "Yes," but I was having difficulty saying it because of the choking. I coughed and repeatedly say, "Yes". Mother pleaded for dad to stop, but he seemed not to care in doing so. Mother pleaded, "Please, stop it already, have mercy on your son. You are so brazen and the neighbors are sleeping already." Father answered her back like he really wanted everyone to hear: "I don't care about the neighbors, and I don't care if they are sleeping already or not, and, and this is my thing, it is not their business!" Mother tried to appeased dad, but to no avail. When I say neighbors, I mean wall to wall. We can literally hear our next door neighbor's snores at night. My mother talked soft and in a very nice way, she said, "I know it's not their business… but please be considerate, it's too late already." You can hear some of my uncle was insulting my dad by pretending they were talking to someone else, but they were actually talking about my dad and his attitudes towards us. These are just few of the instances that I can share, but I'm sure my siblings have their own nightmare with dad, even until the day he (my dad) was 6 feet underneath, my dad was never been forgiven by a sibling.

It was Election Sunday at church that day, and I saw my dad was nominated as a deacon of our church. Can you believe that? I did not know if I would be proud of him or ashamed because his life at home was opposite and different when he was at church. My dad was acting spiritual when at church like he don't come home drunk on Sunday night, he don't yell at us or beat us and disrespected our mother in front of us. But such attitude, complicated lifestyle, and disturbing behaviour had its roots. He was sometimes out of control. My dad got married before World War II. They were very wealthy in Iloilo and his parents spoiled them. My dad's parents made so much money and they had properties. They sent him to school and they have money and food on the table every day. Then the war broke out, and the whole family went to Mindanao to escape the Japanese and the evil of War. They thought it was safer for them to be in Mindanao. His parents changed their last name from Sumagaysay to Sagansay. It changed their lives too. They became so poor after losing everything during the war. His life, his family, and everything in them was never been the same after the ordeal. When his parents passed away, his life has changed at the same time. During our times with him, it was with disappointment, hate, anger, and violence. That was the kind of life he has before he married my mother until I left Bacolod City.

My Brothers Were in Trouble

My siblings' names and profession from the oldest to the youngest were; Rosendo (deceased) a pastor, teacher, professor, and musician. Antonio is a professional tennis player. Samson is a pastor and evangelist. Remigio is a professional tennis player, lawn tennis coach and trainer. Aidariza is a plain housewife. Joram (deceased) took care of our mom in her old age. Ephraim is also a pastor, teacher, writer and an excellent musician. Gideon (deceased) was a pastor as well and lawn tennis trainer.

It was at night in the alley, and almost all of my buddies were drinking booze. It was dark, but everyone was having fun. I was asked to sing, and I did. I sang John Denver's songs, Dan Hill's songs, and Basil Valdez's songs, and other popular Filipino songs of the 70's. I remember my older brother Samson was just looking at my aunt's husband, but my aunt husband was not pleased and happy by the way my brother looked at him. Right there, the fight and trouble started. As a teenager, I was so aggressive that I was ready to break the bottle and use such as a weapon not thinking of what may happen to me and to the victims if it did happen.

My brother may have been with bad guys, and I very well know that Samson had a drinking session with many of his friends every time he comes home late. They were the gang of drunken masters. Yea, that's what I thought of them because of how they spent their income for booze. Samson has many friends and enemy as well. He shared to me how few gang leaders, the tough guys, influential people and politicians in our city and province operates. He knows many of them, and they were subtle, he said. People who accept bribes for a little work that were done for others that they themselves know that those were against the law of the land. This was before the then president Ferdinand E. Marcos declared Martial Law in 1972. I was wondering it could have been the reason why he entered politics in his early years.

Our father has a very high expectation of us. He wanted us all to finish college, but he did not know how to get help, so we all could go to college. Education becomes secondary to my dad. What he instilled in us instead was to hate people and be rude to him. Our father induced to us the wrong perspective, the wrong way of life, and led us to the wrong direction. My aunt who already passed away few years ago once was sharing this to me about how dad had been feared in their village when they were still young. My mom is very beautiful, but no one dared to court her or date her when they heard that she was my dad's girl already for fear of my dad. My dad was a womanizer, too. My aunt said that my dad had 4 girlfriends all at the same time while he was with my mother. That's exactly what my dad wanted me to be too, a gangster and a womanizer. Remember dad's favourite phrase; "It is better to kill than be killed". These kinds of lifestyle is not godly, was not in love, and not very forgiving.

I remember waking up in the morning, and my dad greeted me with these words and with a smile in his face and said; "I heard you slept with a girl last night in your room." It was a room I shared with my 5 siblings. She was a prostitute in a nearby club, and my dad was not mad at me if she slept with me? I was a minor at those times. I was between 16 to 17 years old, and it was fine with him. That's how complicated our home is at that time. Just in our door steps were drinking sessions, gambling, prostitution, etc. I believe that would make anyone understand why it was like that and why it was fine with my dad to sleep with a prostitute. Whether it was a joke or a serious question for him, I assumed may be because my dad was not a Christian, and he was living in sin himself. My dad had no Biblical or highly spiritual standard. He was a compromiser and had double spiritual standard. The reason I said that was because of his lifestyle, his drunkenness, he was not mad when he found out a girl slept in our room, and how he treated us with violence and verbal abused. May be the church during those times did not know anything about what was going on in our home.

When we were drinking with our buddies, you will hear conversations such as this: "We're sorry to hear about that Samson; your dad is abusive to you all." "Yea Sam, we know your father." "He is really tough and abusive; we know that." You will also see some of the people we were drinking with would placed all their weapons on the top of the table for the gang to know what weapons they will all be bringing and what weapon to use if there is a job to finish up or just for protection or just a show off. They have knives, iron bars, chains, and wooden bar the size of two by two by four. It seems that people in that kind of environment are always ready for violence. I have what we called Indian Pana with a 6 inch nail that was made like an arrow.

Have You Noticed the Cycle of Our Lives Living with Our Dad?

Yes, it was like broken records, and it does look like it was a cycle that would never end. We come home late; we get scolded or beaten up. We come home with empty jar at home; we get beat up. We come home with pile of unwashed dishes; we got scolded or beat up. If we come home, and there was no firewood, we will get the same treatment, and it goes on and on…

As young children, if we missed school or we did not wash the dishes or gather firewood for cooking, we will be in trouble with dad, right? Do you imagine living in this generation with that kind of life, and with that kind of upbringing, and with that kind of father? No one in his right mind would ever stay in that state of living and with that father. Not doing your chores means slashes for us by his old leather belt. Yes, in a simple mistake or overlooking of responsibilities and duties as children, the least we could have were demeaning words and loss of self worth. We did not have a stove or gas range or anything electric; therefore, if we come home with no cooked rice or something, it would mean trouble.

'Love' Reminds Me of So Many Christmases with Nothing on the Table

Why 'love' reminds me of so many Christmases with nothing on the table? It was because my mom's tricked and her desire to make us happy on Christmas Day. It's still fresh in my sub-conscious mind of how my mother would show us the socks that she hanged by the window of our house, and told us about Santa Claus who will come to fill those socks with gifts. She will take us to our room and made us sleep in our bed on Christmas Eve. Why? She knows that when the Christmas celebration, the fun, the fireworks, and the noise start to kick in, we have nothing on the table, and we have no Christmas gifts. It is a Filipino custom that everyone gathers around the table with so much food on the table at exactly 12:00 AM on Christmas Eve. They greet each other with a kiss, a hug, and a gift giving. Seldom would we have abundance of food. I was thankful to our neighbours and relatives for their charity for us on Christmas days and New Years' Day.

Waking up with just an apple in our socks because our parents can't afford to buy us toys, new clothes or anything we like to have on Christmas is unforgettable. I remember sometimes on Christmas Eve, we have so much food on our table. Yes, so much food that were given to us by our relatives and neighbors. I remember it on All Saints Day as Filipino custom and tradition, my mother and grandmother would prepare some sticky rice and other food to sacrifice to the dead, with candle and decorations.

However, on Christmas, it was taken so lightly by my parents and grandmother because they were unbelievers at those times or may be due to poverty. One thing is for sure— on Christmas Eve and Christmas Day, my dad would be drunk but a little nicer.

What was the atmosphere at home? It was a little nicer, peaceful, and a little different from other days. But even though my dad was drunk, he did behaved himself. The sad part, we were never made felt he loves us by a kiss, saying to us with a big hug "Merry Christmas, we love you…" I remember my mother at times she would give us a hug or a kiss. It never happened to my dad, even on Christmas day or New Year's Day.

Christmas in the United States is not as fun as it is in the Philippines. Believe it or not, every September 1, the mall and some radio stations are already playing Christmas Carols. It would be from September to first week of January the following year; Christmas music and decors are still alive and still on the wave. Nonetheless, there are few times that it becomes a sad and pity moment for me because I see many children enjoying their Christmas gifts, and Christmas food and fun, but I don't have any, even a small token from my godparents.

As a little child, I would go to bed with my siblings knowing when I get up on Christmas Eve; we would have nothing on our cotton Christmas tree on the wall of our house. You might be wondering about the 'Cotton Christmas Tree.' It's a Christmas tree made of Cotton that were stick on the wall with homemade glue, and were sprinkled with glitters. One Christmas, we had a branch of the Avocado tree from our next door neighbor that my mother made as a Christmas tree, and with the help of my only sister, they both decorated such with cotton and some kind of Construction paper and Christmas papers. We never had Christmas lights because we never had electricity, not until I was in my twenties. We used lamp made from the peanut butter bottle or some kind of a bottle and used such with kerosene. Therefore, Christmas atmosphere in our home is dead.

Imagine having a neighbor or neighbors with Long Playing Records or Cassette Player playing all day, and celebrating Christmas the whole day with gift giving, food on the table, and drinking. Sometimes, they have dancing, and the whole day and night parties. Then, you look at yourself, and your family having a pity party because you're living in poverty. That was my life as a little kid. I have the choice to hate Christmas and not be blamed because of what I went through as a boy. But I always tried to have fun with friends on Christmas Day. December is the most treasured month for me. I always looked forward to Christmas and New Year. I enjoyed the carolling of which we made money. I enjoyed asking for Christmas gift from the Customers at the tennis club, and I enjoyed the Christmas music. Like my birthday, I don't remember celebrating it with a big party with my family prepared set of food and drinks on the table, or a gift from my parents. I did not see Christmas as a big day of preparation of food, drinks, and gift as well. I am not whining, complaining, or in a blaming game on my parents, specifically on my dad. I am writing this part and letting the whole world know about what I went through so we can learn to appreciate life, and Christmas with what we have.

I don't want you to miss a lot of things and the big turned around in our lives. I felt miserable that I would get drunk with wine or beer in my early age because I was frustrated with my father. During those times, I make Christmas as a drinking day and night because I wanted to get over of my hate, misery, and bitterness on my dad. I would drink and smoke and listen to music as my outlet for my misery. But I love my mom and wanted to be with her even after I ran away from home. Although I love being with my mom, I can't stay because of my dad. If I'll stay, my dad may kill me from beatings and abused or I was afraid I would be the suspect instead of a victim.

I and my cousin at the start of every December, we organized a group of kids to do carolling, so we could have money to buy stuff on Christmas day. We also do car wash, sell candies, and sell paper bags at the Bacolod Plaza. The people during those times were busy with Christmas shopping, and they go to a nearby church next to the city park. I believe this is one of the reasons why I hated the attitude of whining and complaining because I know what it means to live a miserable life, and a life with nothing but just the gift of life.

I was also sickly when I was growing up. They call me in our village "Beke-on and Bitokon". What it means is "I have lump on my neck" and "I have parasites in my tummy". Indeed, I was, and it was true due to unhealthy environment since our house was in a slum area. It's just so difficult to picture this kind of environment to those who live in developed and industrialized countries. But anyways, I got my scars in my neck because of the infection that I had after I had a surgery due to a very dirty environment. The parasites were from the food I ate, and we had bad and unhealthy habits at home and in the neighborhood. We did not have the pleasure of eating good and nutritious food, and because of it, I grew up very skinny; I was malnourished, and very sickly. I remember I spent sometimes in bed or in a hospital sick at Christmas time.

Stepping Into the Unknown

My trip to Manila when I ran away from home was with mixed emotions. As I stepped into the ship, it was like stepping into the unknown as an eighteen year-old boy. I have never been in a huge ship before, and I have never been to Manila, and I don't know the place, the language, the people, and the culture. Although we are all Filipinos living in the Philippines; each region and province has its own dialect, culture, and lifestyles.

We have been through this (stepping into the unknown) and even the kindergarten on their first day at school knows what it meant to be in an unknown environment. Whether you are just a new graduate, newly-hired or newly-promoted employee, or you just started a new business, you are stepping into the unknown. Therefore, your life is beginning to flow through the journey to something new and uncertain. You are literally stepping into the unknown and at times, it scares you to death. You may have some sleepless nights and nervous breakdown if you're not careful. The point is, I've been there, and I know what it meant to be in that situation. If you've been there, and I assumed everyone been through such scary experiences, you, therefore, definitely know what I meant to be alone and new to the place. However, to start the journey with me, I want you to be cautious of yours because a little mistake could bring you surmountable disaster, and overwhelming nightmares.

I know my girlfriend loves me so much, and I know she was hurt when her parents made such decisions. She tried to hide me from her parents, but I think some of her cousins were the ones who made her parents know about our relationship. I called her on the phone and told her what happened. She asked me: "What really happened to you?" I shared what my dad did to me and what I did to the guy. I said to her; "I told you, my, my father beat me up." Then, we were interrupted. I believe she was trying to hide me from her parents. She said, "Wait let me get something." I was tired, exhausted and in pain. She tried to comfort me.

I was honest to her when I told her I was wanted for beating up a neighbor. My girlfriend can't believe what I did. She may have thought I was just joking, or fooling around, messing up with her or pulling her feet. But it turned out well because I can tell that she was even more supportive of me. She knew that I was more than willing to follow her to Manila.

I lied once to my girlfriend when I said I will bring her to our house. I took her to the neighborhood and had her visit my aunt house because it was big, nice, and better. I told her it was our house because I was very shy to show her our stilt nipa house and full of hole on its roof and wall, with bamboo floor, and does not have a bathroom. I did not even introduce her to my parents. My girlfriend was from a well-to-do family, and I believe she was upset about it. I believe she was hesitant to believe what I just said because I lied to her big time. Well, I was afraid she will dump me if she found out we were very poor. But she said she love me in spite of our economic status.

I asked my girlfriend several times before she left for Manila if we could go 'secretly married' somewhere, either with the judge or mayor of our city, but she refused. I was willing to take the responsibility already because I wanted to get out of our house and start my own family, so I could be away from my father. I love my girlfriend, and that was the main reason I wanted to marry her when I turned 18, and I would really love to be out of the four corners of our house, too. Who would want to live in a home, which is full of hate, swearing, witchcraft, and violence anyway? My girlfriend was older than me. She was already in college when I first met her. Therefore, we were both ready for our new life, but it was interrupted by her parents' plan. In the Philippines, because of the strong family ties, the parents still control the decisions of their children, and sometimes, even when they are married already. Unfortunately, some were still living under their parents' roof even when they are married and have children already, and the sad part is, they are still dependent to their parents.

I Took a Ship, and It was My First Time Riding in a Big Ship, and My First Time to Many Things

I was excited to get to the ship, but at the same time, I was really scared of what was ahead of me. I don't speak Tagalog during those times. I only speak Ilonggo and a little of Cebuano. I was new to big city and its culture, I don't know anyone, and I don't have a place to live. I prepared myself already that one day I might be homeless. If I can't find my cousins and my girlfriend in Manila- for sure, I will be homeless. I was ready. I did not know what to do in the humongous ship. Thankfully, my doctor friend who took me with him was there to assist me until we get to Manila and find my girlfriend's place. I really appreciate my doctor friend who was very supportive of me. He did not know I was pursued by the law in Bacolod City. It was a mixed emotion for me because I was having a good time in the ship, but at the same time, I was very scared of what may happen to me in Manila, and I know I was not in good terms with my father and many friends in our province because I beat up someone for no reason. I was wanted by the law, but I never knew I was wanted in the whole city and probably, the whole province. I thought it was just in our community.

After my almost 24 hours of first ship ride was my first taxi, jeepney, and tricycle ride in Manila. It was so different; I felt different, and everything was different.

I was still in the Philippines, but the atmosphere of the big city was so peculiar for me. I felt awkward and in my senses, I looked at the Tagalogs like the aristocrats. I felt like I just got off from the jungle in the mountains as a tribe man and started meddling with the New York's executives and the rich and famous. It was also my first time to have slept in a room just by myself, and living in a very nice house with a nice bathroom, nice kitchen, and everything I saw in the house was just so nice. It was my first time to sleep in a bunk bed in my girlfriend's uncle's house just by myself in the room. I noticed like there was a huge changed in my environment and in my new horizon. I felt like I just got out of Egypt with Moses and the Israelites, and I was not a slave anymore. I was a slave of abuses and fear of my father and a slave of my own anger, hate, bitterness, and resentment every time I see him.

I am now in my journey with a new ship. It was a ship of nowhere and uncertainty. I never planned to take a journey that will make me a servant and a slave of the worst thing in my world since my life at the tennis court. My first journey was in Pasay, Manila. I was in a bakery where I started working with the help of my girlfriend. I've never been employed. Now, I am an employee where I've seen the different kind of sinful things in that place. It went from bad to really worst. I believe I was better off if I stayed in the bakery.

When I took my first step toward my dream in the night club where my boss at the bakery moved me to her brother's club, it was there that I see the things I did not see in the Tennis Club and in the Cabaret in Bacolod City.

Working in the so-called Disco Pub which was actually a prostitution den and a gay bar was unbelievable. It was there that I was trapped in the mud and in a quick sand of sin, of hopelessness and despair. I saw 12-year-old girl dancer and all the corruption in the government being dealt with in this Disco Pub. I saw priests, actors, movie directors, and one night fun with same sex, opposite sex, and all kinds of sin. It was indeed a ship headed for destruction.

Night Life in a Disco House

This is how my life started in the Disco Pub. My boss at the bakery gave me a car ride with her. She asked her driver to drive us down to the Disco Pub of his brother for my new job description; but actually the same function-janitor and dishwasher. We arrived early for orientation. The night came and I was in my new job, and the moment of my miserable journey kicked in. The music was loud, the live band was playing, the customers were having fun, the wait staff were all busy, the kitchen were all filled with orders, and everyone was having fun.

I and the floor manager were walking together, and I was being introduced to the club employees. The manager pointed to me the owner of the club who was drinking and eating with his friends. I was given an orientation and the whole functions of the club. After all the instructions, I started working hard. I did everything to please the manager and my boss. I washed all the dishes; I mopped the floor. I tried to clean up the kitchen and the restrooms, and all the windows and surroundings even on day time. I worked as dish washer and janitor for a few months.

One night, I almost hit the guy on his shoulder while I was walking out of the kitchen. He stared at me, and I looked at him like I had an expression of disliked at him. I did not know he was feeling and thinking the same as I do. In my curiosity, I inquired about him to a friend because, at that time, he was talking to my best friend, the cashier of the club. He, then, explained to me that he was my boss' friend, and the notorious man who had been wanted for murders, including killing of law enforcers. His name was Ben Tumbling, and I did not know he was Ben Tumbling until the gentleman who was very close to our boss gave me a clue and all the information about this man. My best friend told me that Ben Tumbling did not like me either. He also asked my friend about me, and my friend told him that I was our boss' favorite worker. I never expect that this man will sleep in a room with me and some other guys. Few days after I met him, we heard the news that he was set up and was killed. One day, I found a lot of empty shells of 45 caliber in the bowl. I just ignored it because it was already in the bowl anyways. I believe those were from him.

My Diligence Pays Off

And because of my diligence, my boss was pleased and happy of my performance that he asked me to sit next to him one night at the club. I was ushered by the manager to the owner's table, but while I was waiting with a loud but beautiful music in the background, my tummy was crumbling for nervousness. I thought I was really in trouble because of what I did to Ben or because I looked at him (Ben) like I wanted to punch him or something. I just kept on waiting and trying not bother myself. I was restless, nervous, and anxious. I was thinking that my boss might ask me about the empty shells, or I may have done wrong that may have upset the boss. After a while, the boss came and talked to me right away while he was still from the distance. I stood up. He said; "Boklit…" I answered nervously; "Boss, I, I don't know about…" My boss said; "How are you? How do you like working here?" Again, I answered nervously and I started to stutter again; "I'm, I'm go-good boss. I like, I like working he-here boss. Thank-thank you so much boss." My boss replied; "Good, have a seat. I am going to promote you as a waiter. There will be no more mopping, cleaning the restrooms, washing the dishes, and other things you're doing right now. You will get a good pay and the tips. You are a good employee, and we will give you what you deserve." I said; "Thank, thank you, boss. I, I…" My boss did not let me finished what I was about to say. He said; "You're good, welcome. Now, go back to what you were doing."

I left so happy, and I tried to hold my excitement until I reached the men's quarter. When I came out of the Disco House, I shouted with so much enthusiasm that I caught my co-workers' attention. The men's quarter was just adjacent to the Pub. Everyone started asking me about the good news that I had. Everyone can't believe I was promoted that fast from dishwasher and janitor to waiter. Although the supervisor and the manager became my drinking buddies and eventually my best friends, I believe it was the trust of my boss to me that made him that decision.

My boss did not expect me to fail him on my first night as a waiter. I was trained during day time on what to do and what to expect as a waiter. I was given all the information about the wine, the beer, the foods and the details on the hostesses as well as the dancers, and the corruption in business. When the manager told me; "Now, Boklit it's time to put this into practice." That night in Disco Club, my life began to stir up for something I thought would really be the start of the dream I've been longing to embrace, and that is to be an entertainer in Japan. While working as a janitor and dish washer, every night as I watched the band playing and the singers on the stage, I can see myself in Japan. Back on my first night at the Disco Pub as a waiter, it was not as expected of me, and it was not as I expected it to be.

That night in a Disco Club, I picked up my first order to be served to my first customers. It feels great with my uniform on as a waiter. As I took my first tray of the customers' orders; I nervously and excitedly rushed to the table of the group of gentlemen with the hostesses around the table that works in that Disco Club to entertain the customers. Everybody was having fun drinking.

When I was about to place their orders on the table, I grabbed the beer over from my shoulder in the tray. Unfortunately, everything slipped from the tray and dropped on the floor and the table. Some dropped on the lap of the customers and the hostesses. It was indeed disastrous for me, to the ladies, and the customers. They all got wet and were very mad at me that one of them even wanted to punch me. One of the customer yelled at me; "What are you doing!?" The lady from the club pushed the customers' anger when she said; "What a mess... Do you know what you're doing?" I heard cursing and swearing, and all kinds of profanity, but still I kept on saying I'm sorry. One of the customers wanted to punch me, but I was ready to lost that job, I was ready to fight back. "I'm going to punch you!" he said.

The disaster that I made caught the attention of the supervisor, the manager, and the owner. Everyone's eyes were on us. It also made all the customers and workers stopped what they were doing, and just watched us. In spite of the noise of the music, the commotion, and the crowd being so loud at the time; it just caused everyone to be quiet and watched us. I was embarrassed, scared, and confused on what to do next. The customer stood up and yelled; "What do you want to prove huh!?" I just respectfully and nicely say; "I'm sorry, sir."

The spot in the club where it happened is still fresh in my mind. I can still see it from my conscious mind, and how the beers, the Ice bucket, and all the glasses slide down while I was reaching for the beer. I told them it was my first night but still one of the customers pushed me, grabbed me on my chest and pushed me on the wall and yelled at me. I said; "I'm sorry, I don't mean to do it; it's my first night, and it was just an accident." He yelled at me; "Shut up!" I was already tempted to start the war. Thankfully, the manager came to my rescue and helped me up. The manager tried to settle down the customer. Give them everything for free to ease up their anger. I dashed off my shirt and left straight to the kitchen. I untied my neck tie, grabbed my cigarettes from my pocket and smoke outside the Disco House.

I was called to the boss' office and was scolded by my boss and the manager. My boss, although he was very angry already, he tried to understand me and explained to me the technique. My boss was nice and good looking. You can't really feel his anger and disappointment because he was pleasant to talk with. He told me; "You know I trusted you. You know I am very helpful to you. Boklit, I want the best for you, and that's the reason why I give you this job. You messed it up, and I don't know what to do this time." I apologized and promised him that I will do better next time. I said; "I'm so, so, sorry boss, it, it really was an accident." My boss delivered the bad news to me in his office when he said; "I'm sorry, but I have no choice, I have to give you a week of suspension. It means you will go through strenuous job training without pay." I was discouraged, but I took it as a challenged.

The next day, I filled up the empty bottles with water and put them in the tray and pretended that I was serving the customers in a busy place. I was trained on day time and made to work without pay outside the Disco Club helping and cleaning. Because I was idle and discouraged, I started to drink more, smoke more, and became bitter in my life and father. I blamed him for what happened to me at that time.

One night while I was very restless, I was trying to sleep but I can't sleep. I started reading the letters my brother Ephraim sent me while he was in the seminary. I was supporting him in his seminary time. That night I picked up one of his letter to me and started reading it. It was all about God, about having peace with God, and satisfaction in life. He always shared to me the gospel in his letters, and gave me Bible verses. I read them one by one. It was a boring birthday for me until this happened…

My First Big Birthday Celebration and All the Disaster in the DJ Booth

After the Disco Club closed its door for the night, and I was at the men's quarter in the room just by myself, I heard a knock on the door. The manager called me; "Boklit! Boklit!" I opened the door and said; "Hmmm… what are you doing here? It's 4 in the morning." The manager replied; "I know I'm sorry to wake you up." I asked; "What's up? What's going on?" The manager said; "Boklit, the boss wants to see you." I asked in my mind with a big wonder of 'why'? I then softly asked the manager; "Why?" The manager smile at me and said; "I don't know." If you are in my shoes you can already tell what I felt while I was walking down to his office. You can definitely read my mind by placing yourself on mine. "Is he going to fire me or get me out of here? Does it has something to do with my attitude at the training yesterday?"

I changed my clothes while the manager turned her back as not to see me changing my clothes. I asked; "Am I in trouble or something?" The manager answered; "You're always been in trouble, and your life is a mess. So what are you worried and talking about?" I replied to her, I was extremely nervous; "I know, I know, what I mean is, is he going to, to kick me out of here for, for good?" The manager was trying to encourage me, and said; "Just get ready and be there, the boss don't have all the time for you. Relax and be yourself, okay!"

The manager and I went, and it was because they wanted to give me a surprise birthday party. I was fortunate to have bosses and managers who were nice and understanding. It was the first time in my life to celebrate my birthday with so much food and drinks. They gave me "sky is the limit". For the first time in my life, a group of people sang Happy Birthday song to me. The manager started to shout "Happy Birthday!" They also played the song. It was indeed a Happy Birthday, and I shared to them that it was my first birthday party in my whole lifetime. It was my 20th Birthday. The boss and some of the staff were there.

Everyone was happy, singing and seeing me so happy. I was so emotional. I tried to control my emotion, but it was so obvious, and it was kind of uncontrollable for me already. I've never been so drunk in my whole life but that day. I believe I did something crazy that day because I was so drunk, that I can't say it in public, and I am so ashamed of myself even until now.

My boss greeted me first and everyone at the club. It's nice to hear almost for the first time in my life, aside from the church people who would say words like "Happy birthday, Boklit, and we want to let you know we care for you." They also wanted me to share a few words before we eat and drink without limit. Yes, it was without limit. I shared to them that I never had a cake for my birthday since I was little. I never had a blast or a birthday party like this with food and drinks. I look at my boss and personally said to him in front of the team; "Thank you so much for, for… boss for this special treat. Since I was a, a kid, I don't remember, cell- celebrating my birthday even with just a little party. I don't, I don't remember my parents throw a birthday party for me or, or for my siblings. We were very poor, hence, no, no food, no drinks, no gift, no hug and kisses, and, and I'm not suggesting you all kiss me. Thank you so much. Boss, you're different…" Obviously, every time I was nervous, excited or angry- my stutter kicks in. Everybody laugh, and some made a joke and gestures of kissing me. Some of the ladies kissed me and gave me a hug. I was never been so happy such as this special day. The boss tried to get everyone's attention. "Let's have a toss for Boklit, and let's have fun!" We did, and I felt so happy and special that day. Everyone did have fun. They all eat, drink, and were merry. It was a very memorable day for me. I can't forget the 'El Grande' celebration.

One special day for me, my boss made an

announcement; "Boklit, I am going to promote you as assistant to our DJ today. He will train you and after the training, you will start working with him. For now, you work as a waiter until you are ready to be a DJ. There will be no more glass and beer breaking for you. For the mean time, you will have to work part time on both jobs."

Working as DJ was the beginning of misery or it was God's work for my salvation? I wear my new hat with a new job description, and a headphone in my head at the DJ booth. I love music, and I love what I was doing. Playing music the whole night was really fun. I can do tripping and at the same time working. Tripping was the street term for a person addicted to marijuana or drugs who desired and wanted to feel the kick of such. It is when they get high and began hallucinating or tripping. When they get bad trip, it means trouble. I will talk about that "trouble" that happened to me on the next chapter.

One night, in the booth, while I was playing the disco music for the customers to dance on the dance floor, a dancer knocked on the door of the booth, and I opened the door for her. She introduced herself and gave me some instructions with regards to the music she wanted me to play for her slot. This very beautiful young dancer said, "Hello, my name is Jenny (not her real name), and I will be performing on the 3rd slot, and here is my music." Jenny handed me the 45 records by Boney M entitled 'Felicidad' to be played during her scheduled slot.

Jenny was about to say something when a drunk gentleman (a customer in the club) interrupted us. Jenny; "Hey, I…" The customer; "Hello beautiful, excuse me, can I have dance with you? Can I make a request Mr. DJ?

Can you play slow music? I wanted to have a sweet dance with her." Jenny; "Oh I'm sorry, not right now." She left looking at him with a smile, and gave him a very seductive look. I just looked at them back and forth.

Not after long the customer came back; "Are you alright Mr. DJ tonight?" I respectfully answered; "Yes I am, sir." Customer; "I want you to play YMCA instead." I said; "No, not right now sir. The dancers has, umm, have their own music that they, they wanted to dance with… and, and may be later after their slot time." The customer began to get mad at me, and said; "You have a choice; play it or eat it!" He tried to get in inside the booth, and I stopped him and said; "Are you threatening me? Get out of my booth!" The customer was surprised I said that, but at the same time he was very angry. The people and the staff, waiters, and the manager noticed that I and the big man were arguing inside the booth. The Big man, the customer arrogantly shouted at me and pushed me hard on the side. I angrily shouted back and told him to wait till I get done with the dancers, and we can settle it outside the club, not inside the booth.

I confronted him; "What is your problem man, get out and let us settle this outside! Or get out of my booth and I'll, I will play your music." I knew I could never win with the big man in fist fight; but I was thinking that my tricked to some of the people I hurt in the province might work again. This time I was thinking of using the folding chair. I checked and looked at the folding chair by the side of the door while challenging him. The customer began to be so annoying to me and very persistent. He was so drunk, and I was thinking I can handle him without the chair and the cheater's tricked. I can tell by his body and head being so unbalanced when he moves and talked. "No! You play it first, then, we will do it." I yelled at him; "No! Now get out of ma-my booth because I'm no, not playing your song!" He tried to touch and grab me with his hand but I resisted and yelled at him. "Don't touch me again, be-because I'm not scared of you and, I am not working for you!" I looked at him with a tiger looks and in anger. He was mad too and shouted at me; "You are really trying to annoy me and challenging me, you bones…!" I smiled at him; "Try me out…!" He then pulled his gun from his waist and pointed it in my head. I said; "Now I know the, the reasons why you, you're brave; you're drunk, you are bigger than me, and you have a gun!" His gun was still pointing on my head, he yelled at me; "Shut up or I will blow your head off!" I said; "Go ahead, pull the, the trigger or you can go with, with me outside and have a square with me. You are bigger than, than me, you should not be afraid to, to have a fist fight with me. Let's settle it outside!" This man did not know that I was suicidal during those times because of the misery and the hate I have in my heart.

The manager, the staff, the waiters all came around us and asked him to surrender his gun or he will face the consequences before he can even pull the trigger. My best friends talk to him and gave him the ultimatum. My best friend the supervisor who was also a big man talked to him and told him; "You may put down Boklit tonight, but remember, we will not let you touch the ground of the hospital or jail. Surrender your gun to our manager and we will let you go with your gun outside with the security.

You know what I mean; we will not let you get out of this booth alive or in 50/50 condition." He agreed, and he gave his gun to the manager. This man made a hands up and gave up the gun and he said; "Alright! Alright! I will give it to you!"

Everyone started to clear the door of the booth. We found out that the man was part of the regular customers that was from the Philippine Custom. Back in those days the abused of power were prevalent in the whole country and in many departments of the government. The manager and the guards and waiters escorted him out. The manager promised to give it back to him outside. They told him that they will give it back to him in his car outside. "The security will be there waiting for us with your gun. But I will hand it over to you in your car. No police records for you, and I will discuss it to Boklit, as his manager." As the manager was giving him the assurance, all the bouncers and the staff helped him exit the booth to the parking area. Then the manager went back to the booth and talked to me in the booth.

Another scolding session in my boss' office due to what I did. The boss and I had a talked in his office again. He made me understand why he called me to his office this time. "I understand the manager talked to you about what happened last night. Partly, you were right, but you should have talked to the manager or your supervisor before it heats up. You have an anger problem Boklit." I have a mannerism; I scrubbed and pinched my nose when I talked or was idle. I respectfully answered my boss while rubbing and touching my nose like I was so rude to him; "Yes, I was very angry with him, and I, I know I have anger problem. I hated those who, who bully, abused, and was mean to me. That's when my anger boiled in."

My boss inquired; "Tell me Boklit, what really happened?" I started sharing to him my life in the province. I believe poverty, pain, abusive father, broken family, hate, there is no love at home. Those things contributed to what I used to be... as I paused. Despite these, I also shared to him my positive plans for my life. You can tell that there were struggles that existed and were active in my life, in my mind, and in my heart. But, at the same time, I was dreaming and wanting to look forward or be futuristic. I believe I was lost, and I did not know what to do.

> *"Proverbs 27:1 KJV Boast not thyself of tomorrow; for thou knowest not what a day may bring forth." Tomorrow is one thing that we don't know, but we can only think of it positively and dream about it day by day. It is sometimes totally black and dark, filled with hopelessness and distress; but we can always look at it differently, and in God's perspective, and with God's blessed hope. In "James 4:14 KJV Whereas ye know not what shall be on the morrow. For what is your life? It is even a vapour, that appeareth for a little time, and then vanisheth away." The Bible says;"Luke 13:33 KJV Nevertheless I must walk to day, and to morrow, and the day following: for it cannot be that a prophet perish out of Jerusalem. Matthew 6:30 KJV Wherefore, if God so clothe the grass of the field, which to day*

> *is, and to morrow is cast into the oven, shall he*
> *not much more clothe you, O ye of little faith?"*

I know everything I planned, whatever I say, and wrote were all wrong and unacceptable in terms of killings and robbing a bank. But you know when you're lost and do not have God and the Holy Spirit in your life, selfishness and bad decisions in life can often be part of your nature.

The evil heart, evil desires, and the evil plans that I have had were disgusting and unacceptable to God and man. I was ashamed and I am so ashamed just to think of all about those evil things that were in my heart. What happened? How come I am still here? How come I am not dead yet? My mother was a very prayerful woman. I believe that my younger brother and older brothers were praying for me too. I think the Sunday school times I had, the force Bible reading of my brother on me, the religious activities such as feedings of the children from Christian churches all helped developed the fear of God in me.

I was asked by my supervisor and manager about my life and family; "How are your parents doing in your province?" I told them; "They are well, 2 of my, my siblings are now pastors, and 2 are professional tennis players." They said; "Expensive sports such as…" I replied; "We live next to the tennis court, and we, we learned… you know." They asked; "Did you finish school?" I shamefully answered; "I went to, to 5 different high schools, I only finished 3rd year. I, I did not flunked- just lack of, of attendance. I hated school, and I have no motivation. School was so slow for me, I… because I want to be out there making a name and money. I wanted to be famous and, and because I know I was, I was not dumb." They said; "Alright, always keep your cool and don't be quick to get angry, alright, see you tonight. We just want to know more about your life… see you tonight".

It annoys me so much that I raised my voice when I answered back. They stopped the interrogation or late interview. They might just want to know more about me and why I act the way I did. I was outside of the night club in a very nice afternoon and was smoking marijuana with some friends. Some of the ladies came in to work early to prepare for that night show. They invited me to come with them inside the club. I made a gesture telling them I'm finishing my weeds before getting in. They all laughed and gave me a flying kiss.

I went inside after finishing up my weeds. I walked to the booth feeling high and having a good trip after the effect of marijuana. I played the music from the DJ booth, sat down and started my tripping. Some of my favorite things to do while trying to start my tripping were touching my nose, snipping my fingers and closing my eyes trying to feel good. I love the feelings of flying and not feeling any problem or pressure.

When I felt depressed, I would smoke nonstop, drink beers, listen to music and just sit all day until the club opens. I like my mind to take me to my childhood life when I enjoyed playing with my friends and cousins. I take pride of me using an old iron with coals which is being lit with fire and then fanned by me as 10 years old boy. I would think of my grandmother whom I was her favorite grandson. I would watch her doing a witch craft, and my other grandmother would be doing card reading. If it was a bad look which means a bad luck for grandmother. I could think of my mother and sister and other ladies who were doing the spirit of the glass. They talked about death and some of the people who've already been gone before us.

I would also reflect my life in a small church, and refreshed the Bible study in a small church. One of the most impactful and really fresh in my sub-conscious mind was my flash back of the Indian street preacher in Bacolod plaza who preaches about the second coming of the Lord Jesus Christ. I was very disturbed and have been interrupted by my hate and recollection of my dad's brutality and lacked of love. I can hear my father yelling at me and knocking on the door and was very angry.

This has happened to me several times while working as a DJ. Outside the door of the DJ's booth was my best friend knocking at the door. My tripping was interrupted by my best friend's knocking on the door of the booth. I opened the door, let him in, and I just went back from my hallucinations and tripping like I did not see him. But I lost it all. When he started talking, I lost my focus on my tripping that I see him as an enemy in a blink of an eye. In my anger and disappointment, I started kicking and punching him but he did not fight back. He was actually asking me to have dinner with him because he will buy me one, but because I was distracted, I began to have a bad trip. My friends were very understanding of me. This friend got out of my booth and did not say anything to me until the next day when I was in my right mind.

In one instance, my other friend did the same. When

I opened the door, my friend was on the door smiling, but I saw it like he was very mad. In my hallucination and tripping while my friend was calling my name; I felt like my friend was pouring water on me when I was looking at the beautiful sky, and I was there floating. They said I did not move my head and was just focused on the rotating disco ball. It was all related to me the following day by my friends. The reasons why I shared this, it is to show to everyone who were hooked or may want to try marijuana and other drugs for the fun of it that it is not fun but a nightmare and very destructive.

My manager at the office slammed the folder with the name "BOKLIT" at the front of it. It was a report about the incident at the booth. "My goodness, you're back in my office again. I can't believe you're, you're like at the Dean's office every day or week. What's wrong with you? I thought you are going to be good this time?" When the manager angrily confronted me in his office, I was about to say something; "Boss, you…" The manager interrupted me; "Stop it now! I placed you at the booth with our boss blessings so that… so that all you have to do is to deal with music and records. Boklit, all you did was taking drugs and smoking marijuana." I plead for him and he gave me another chance. He said; "Alright, you seemed to be a tough guy for me and causing so much trouble here at the club, I am going to give you a new responsibility. You will work as a DJ and if short with waiters, you will be working as waiter, and at the same time you will work with the bouncers solving their troubles with the annoying, trouble makers, and the 1-2-3 customers (it means the customers who does not pay) and drunk customers. Now get out of my office." When I was about to close the door, the boss said; "Boklit, no deadly weapons with you."

Boklit of a Thousand Faces

Who "Boklit" really is? It was a big question to many of my friends and siblings. I have been in question of who really Boklit to my love ones, to my friends, and to my co-workers, and to church people.

I was living a life of different faces. I was very loyal friend to my close friends and co-workers. I was very loyal to my boss, to my supervisor, to our floor manager and general manager, as well as to the ladies who works at the Disco Club. I was so bad to others especially to people whom I don't like their faces, the way they walk or talk, and if they have an arrogant gesture and by the way they act or conduct themselves. I also have a violent attitude towards innocent people. On Sundays, when I visit the church, I act like I'm the holiest person under the roof of the chapel. I was becoming like my dad when I was at church. I lived a different life and lifestyle from Monday through Sunday at 9:00 AM, then after church, I will be a different person. I wear a holier-than-thou mask when I go to the protestant church along Taft Avenue, Manila. I was very nice to a few ladies but hated the rest of the attendees.

I love my mother, siblings, and some of my friends, but I hated my dad, some of my co-workers, and those whom

I don't like. I was destroying my life and at the same time I had big dreams. Since I moved from the bakery to the Disco Pub, my girlfriend did not want to see me again. I worked hard finding an opportunity to work abroad. I applied in many agencies for work but was turned down. My background was checked and I was very low in terms of my status as being a good citizen obviously.

What people said about me during those times? When asked what they think of Boklit, people said; "His educational attainment was not acceptable either." "He grew up in a very dysfunctional family." "Boklit grew up in a very complicated family with abusive father." "Boklit is very funny, I remember we were watching a movie, it was a comedy. So everybody laughed at a scene, then when it was already quiet and everybody stopped laughing already- Boklit laughed so loud that he made everyone laughed during a very serious and intense scene." "He is alcoholic, a smoker (I smoked more than a pack each day), drug addict (to atevan, cough syrups, marijuana, etc) I've watched some of his friends who smoked marijuana with him and do drugs died of accidents, suicide, mentally ill, or end up in jail, but Boklit is violent." "He is a nice guy and very loyal to his friends." "Funny, smart, but weird though." Those are some of the statement I heard from my friends.

Although I was a funny guy to my friends, my family issues, and growing up in a dysfunctional family made it more complicated and abnormal for me. I grew up being in Sunday school for almost every Sunday in a small Baptist church in Bacolod City, yet it just adds up to my confusion on spirituality due to my father's bad testimony.

129

I felt like I was living in a very complex world. I was raised to pray, force to read the Bible by my big brother Samson, and go to church on Sundays. However, it did not have a big impact right away. It seemed a tinkling cymbal to me because all those things that I religiously practiced did not really pinned me down to the truth and love of God and for God due to what was going on inside our house.

My New Job at the Disco Club at Night was the Worst of All Jobs I had in Manila

Taking care of the unruly and drunk customers was not a good idea. I was called to help settle down the drunk and unruly customer at the table of one of the hostess. The customer wanted to touch the private parts of the hostess. The hostess complained, and I talked to the customer but the customer was rude and resistant. I picked him up from the table and dragged him outside and told him to go. I then went back to the table to talk to his friends who were then was scared of what I did to their unruly friend.

At one time, a customer was trying to get some physical touch with the girls. The girl whisper to me of what the customer was doing and I talked to them of which the customer agreed with, and cooperated. It was good if they do like that, it saves me from big trouble. I don't have any idea why a skinny guy would always be called by a supervisor of the club to take care of the troublemakers inside a Disco Pub. At one point, my boss at one of the corner of the pub was watching me when I dealt with the customer, and gave me a thumb up for doing a good job.

I remember a group of thugs came in and ordered so much food and drinks. They also asked for ladies. Their orders made everyone doubt. The waiters and staff were all alerted by these customers' attitude at the table. They all have fun and they ate with the ladies. Everyone in the club knows their intentions, and that is to run away from the bills. They planned it well and meticulously thought of it and make it looked like they can really get away or slip away without paying the bills. Again, it put me in a lot of dangers, and beating the intoxicated customers who refused to pay. My supervisor and I planned it well on how we can peacefully, and nicely executing it without creating chaos inside the pub.

We alerted the security, the waiters, and all the staff. These non paying customers were tagged as the '1-2-3 guys'. The '1-2-3 guys' meaning they count from 1 to 3 then run from their responsibilities or duties to pay or settle their bills. The first guy went to the restroom and then leave going out. The second guy walked by the side of the building then out to the main door trying to leave the building unnoticed. The last one asked the waiter that he is going to get some fresh air outside. But the waiter stopped him, and I came in to their conversation and said; "Sir, sorry you can't get out right now." The customer inquired; "Why? Do you have problem with me? You know I can always get out of here anytime I wanted to, right?" I joined the conversation; "Your Buddies went that way, the other on that way, and you are about to go that way. We know your tricks and your planned exit, and it is to come out and make your way to escape from paying the bills."

The customer this time is more unruly, resistant, and arrogant. He talked to me like he wanted to intimidate me; "Are you stupid? You don't know me, do you? You don't know who you are dealing with." The customer was very upset and restless. He tried to runaway but I ran after him and tackled him and put him on the ground, and pinned him there. He was on his face down on the ground and pinned him down until I get some help.

The bouncers and waiters started to follow and beat up the customer. One of my co-workers grabbed the knife from the customer, but I embraced the customer and protected him. I was almost stabbed to death by my co-worker if I did not shout out loud; "Stop!" My co-worker asked; "Who said stop" It got everybody's attention. I was on the top of the man, I turned my face up and said; "No one will hit this man again or I will be your worst nightmare. I want everyone to stay out of this man. He is mine. He is your gift to me." I stood up, wiped the dirt on my pants and shirt, picked up the beaten up customer and told him to seat. My friends and co-workers started backing off and wondering and talking to each other about the different attitude I was beginning to adopt. It was because I felt something was missing inside. I was also sick and tired of violence in my life.

I had that conscience and conviction that I felt inside of me. I can't explained it but some of my friends talked to each other such as; "What's wrong with Boklit?" "What is he doing? He almost got killed for defending the customer." "Boklit is weird." "Is he alright?" "I can't believe he tried to stop us… why'd he do that?" The supervisor asked; "Why did you do that to the customer? He tried to kill you with this knife, and I almost killed you. He is a cheater! What's wrong with you Boklit?" I suggested, "We can make him sign, sign a note and let them all, all pay instalments of … or, or one payment. The boss I'm sure will agree." The staff said; "You put yourself in danger." I told them; "I know, but he has enough already." Some said, "It was the scariest part of the night; you were on the top of the customer and everyone wants to take part in beating him."

Every time I was at the booth playing some Disco music, and watching all kinds of sins around me; I was reminded of the verses from the Scriptures that I memorized from the Sunday school class such as; John 3:16, John 14:1- 6, and the Romans Road. I also had a flashback of the Indian preacher who preaches in Bacolod plaza every day. The message in his briefcase on the sticker which says; "Jesus is Coming Soon! Be Ready." It was so fresh in my mind that I can feel him talking to me right there at the booth, almost every night. Along with all the flashbacks I had, I would start to think of what if Jesus will come today? I don't know if I can be with Him. What if I die today? I was thinking of my brother who is a pastor will help me get there. He can talk to God to let me in… I was really scared to die because I was afraid to stand in the presence of God for all the sins I committed. That emptiness and misery becomes really real to me. It was like the true misery and emptiness that no one ever experienced but me. Not out of hate and bitterness to my dad, but something I can't explain.

I started coming to protestant church in Manila where I met some of the dignitaries and high ranking government officials. Obviously, I did not stay long coming to that church because I felt like I don't fit in. But the more I wanted to do right and get right with God, the more I encountered temptations, struggles and oppositions from the devil.

In one of the table, there was some problem. The waiters were talking to one of the customers. The customer was short of few hundred pesos. The waiters and the staff won't let him leave his table until he would settle down the short. It was less than $10.00 in our money today. I curiously came in into the scene and asked; "What's going on in, in here? The waiter said; "This man is short of his bill." I asked; "How much do you owe?" The man said; "Just less than 500 pesos (less than $10.00) short sir. I'm sorry, I…" He called me sir. I asked; "Are you going to beat up a man for a few dollars short?" The waiter asked; "Boklit, what about…?" I said; "Put that on me, he was honest- no more money." During those times I was making 75.00 pesos a night, and it was a good amount of money for my age during those times, and I was single, plus tips. I don't pay for board and lodging. Therefore, that amount was not a big deal to me. I tapped the man on his back and told him he is free to go. The man was very appreciative to me that he wanted to hug me, but the waiter in charge told him to 'stop that drama'. They all laughed, and I laugh, too. My co-workers and friends started to notice something different in me. I noticed it as well, and I can't just explain it.

Meeting the Indian Preacher Again at the Front of the Night Club in Manila

I don't know if I tagged this as the weirdest, interesting, God's miracle or the Lord Jesus Christ's manifestation in the flesh to me. If you remember when I said that I already felt God was working in my heart through the preaching of the Indian preacher that I heard every time I passed by the plaza, that is where the real story begins. One night, while I was preparing to get out and smoke outside the club, I felt like something was leading me there. That night, I felt weird like I really need to go out. I was so uneasy and was uncomfortable at that time. I knew the air conditioning was cold, but I felt warm inside. The music was loud because I played it loud, and as I watched the atmosphere, it was seems boring and the business was slow. There was no customer. Most of the waiters, the ladies, and other staff were outside smoking and conversing. I felt like someone was pushing me to come out and smoke or something else that I can't figure out or understand what was going on in me. Whatever that something that was forcing me to come out and smoke was part of God's plan. So I went out to smoke outside the Disco House. I could have done it inside the Pub, but it was a weird feeling for me to come out.

I took my cigarettes from my shirt at my left pocket and my lighter from my pants on my right side. I slowly walked down towards the door to come out and smoke. Almost at the same time that this Indian preacher was at door with his black briefcase and saying over and over; "Jesus is Coming Soon! Be Ready." It was the same man, the same briefcase, the same sticker and message, and the same suit that he wear when I heard him preached since I was 9 years old until I left Bacolod city.

To give you an idea, the duration of the flight from Bacolod to Manila is about an hour. It would take you more than 8 hours to drive. It's approximately 300 miles in distance. I was already about 22 years old when this Indian preacher showed up in front and right at the door of the Disco Pub where I was working. If it was not God Himself, or the Lord Jesus Christ, then, it could have been His angel. Or the Indian street preacher was obedient to God's call, to the Holy Spirit and His purpose that he went there not knowing that God had prepared him to catch the Big Fish- yours truly.

When I opened the door of the club, I was startled, surprised, and scared to see the same Indian Preacher. I had a flashback of him listening to him when I was a little boy in Bacolod city. I was stilled, and then backed off a little step. Then I said; "What, what are you, you do- doing here?" When I said those words, I said it with unexplained emotion, with fear and wonder- how in the world did this man know I was there? Is he following me? Was He God or Jesus? The Indian man did not answer my question, but he just kept on preaching. I heard the same message over and over, this time with a little understanding of what this man was saying. Jesus died on the cross for our sins. He loves you and He wants to save you and gave you eternal life in heaven. He gave His life for the forgiveness of our sins. I have no idea if the people and my co-workers were aware of what went on that night at the door of the disco house. I never asked them if they saw that Indian Preacher at the door preaching to me.

My brothers Samson and Ephraim shared the same message to me, and they said they hear him preached the same message from that Indian street preacher every time they passed by where he preached in the Plaza. We celebrate Christmas because one day He came down from heaven by Mary and the miraculous work of the Holy Spirit. We celebrate Holy Week and Easter because one day He died on the cross, He was buried, and rose again the third day according to the Scriptures. Jesus went up to heaven to prepare a place for you. But are you ready to stand in His presence if you die today? He is coming back, but are you ready to be with Him? Your fear of death will diminish if you put your trust in Jesus. You accept Him today, and ask Him to forgive you of your sins. I ignored other voices who were calling me at that time. I turned my back from the Indian Preacher and ran as fast as I can to our quarter. I was scared and restless, and I didn't know what to do. Nevertheless, that unforgettable experienced I had made me closer to the truth of the Word of God. I began to recall the time when I had a dream of falling in the bottomless pit, which leads me to think of someone that is Supreme Being because I was so scared of what may happen to me when I totally fall at the bottom of that dark place.

During that time, I walked back and forth in my room. I was very emotional, and I remembered my brother's letter to me and what I heard from the Sunday school at church, and the Bible study. These are some of the things that popped up in my head when I was in the night club living in fear and misery: The Sunday school teacher leading us in prayer, the church Invitation and evangelistic meetings, the Bible study, the Evangelist, Ephraim's letter, and my mom's prayer and advises.

I fell asleep and never got up 'till late in the morning the next day. I never slept like that before because it was the best sleep I had for a while. I prepared to walk to my favorite restaurant and on my way to the restaurant, I saw this Indian preacher again sleeping on the ground with just the cartons as his bed. He had his briefcase next to him. I just kept on walking and just looked at him. I stopped (and rubbed my nose and sniff) and wanted to say something, but I changed my mind after a while. The Indian preacher just looked at me without a word.

Every time I was at the booth watching the people dance, and the club dancers at the stage with their attire that were not pleasing and actually very sinful in the eyes of man and God. This time I was already convicted and I started to recall the preaching and this man's message from his briefcase. Aside from the verses I heard, I also was hearing some voices which says; "God loves you!" "He dies for your sins" "Jesus is Coming Soon, Be Ready!" "He gave His life for you!" "Would you accept Him now?" I would just get out of the booth and start walking while at the same time I was hearing the voice of a preacher inviting the people to come forward. I heard the preacher says, "He came for you, would you come to Him right now. He laid down His life for you, would you lay down your life and your sins to His feet. If Jesus will come tonight, do you want to be with Him in heaven?" I believe all those things were in my mind but out of my heart.

I assumed the people around me and my friends noticed me like I was thinking so deep. They may have assumed I was on drugs. Whatever may have been in the mind of others was different with what was going on in my mind. I sometimes felt like I wanted to cry but... I felt so miserable and hopeless that I was looking for something to make me happy, take out the fear in my heart- the fear of death and His coming, and the emptiness I had in my heart. I tried visiting the nearby zoo, the nude show across the block, and again drugs and alcohol. I sometimes finished up 2 packs of cigarettes just to entertain myself. When my friends and co-workers asked me if I'm alright, I said; "Yes, I'm, I'm alright." I actually don't even mean it because I was never alright.

Because of what was going on in my life, again, I began to drink so much that I find myself crawling for being so drunk. My friends at one time have to carry me to the taxi and put me down in bed for being so drunk. There were times that I would play a long playing record and got out of the building not remembering my record was done already. Unfortunately, the supposed to be 'turning point' for me to God becomes another bump and struggle for me to get over. I can tell that Satan really wanted to keep me in his fold. The devil would do everything not to get rid of me. He will always send something or someone to stop God from what He was doing in my life. One of the examples of what I mean is this scenario one afternoon in front of the Disco Pub.

While I was walking back to the door of the Disco

Club, I saw the security guard was bullying the kitchen helper at the club. I was back to my former violent attitude again this time.

I came close to inquire; "Is, is everything alright here?" The kitchen helper said; "This security guard is trying to bully me." I asked; "What is he doing to, to you?" Kitchen helper said; "He was asking for money from me, and I told him I don't have money, and then he hit me on my head." I asked the security guard; "Why? And, and why are you do-doing it to him?" I was looking at his gun while I was madly asking the security guard. The security guard responded; "Why? It's none of your business!" I said; "It is now... He, he is my buddy." The security guard tried to touch his gun, but I was faster than him that my hand was already in the holster of his 38 revolver before he tried to grab it. I gave him a snap in the stomach and told him to stop bullying my friend. The security guard was in pain and lost a little strength. I told him; "You, you are trying to be the tough guy here, and, and you pick the wrong man." The security guard while in pain said to me; "You're challenging me?" "No, my friend, just leave him a-alone and apologize to him." The security guard said; "Alright! Alright! Please take off your hand from my gun before it goes off in my feet." I looked at him at his eyes and said; "I, I can let this gun blow off your, your feet and, and not be jailed. I, I will let go, because I want you to, to be my friend, alright, and..." The security guard in agreement said again; "Alright! Alright, please. Ok, I'm sorry." I said; "Agree huh." I slowly let go off of my hand from the holster. The security guard tried to fix his holster, and his shirts. He was still feeling the pain as he rubs his tummy. My friend (the Kitchen helper) thanked me. Everyone who witnessed what I did and the change in my attitude made everyone wondered, what was really going on in my life?

The Bad News Came When I Thought Everything Will Be Fine

The boss was meeting all the workers. The agenda was about the closing of the club for few reasons. The boss announced how it becomes too slow in terms of the customers' stats and orders. The main reason was actually the construction of the railway, which affected the net income of the business. The other reasons could be the national election that was coming where many of our regular customers are campaigning. "We are turning this Club into a Gay Bar after we make some changes on the interior and as we beautify the whole building," the owner said. The good news is, we will not be jobless because there'll be movies to be shot in our facility by famous celebrities. We will be a part of this as a background and, maybe, a part-time crew. Indeed, we became a part of the movie. I've watched the clips on YouTube recently.

At the Rizal Memorial Park, It was My Short Love Story Again

Due to the temporary closure of the Disco Club, I had all the time to relax, to walk and enjoy the day. I did everything I wanted to do when I can't do it when I was still busy at work. I also had the time to enjoy my life and it was including watching movies and sports. I also tried to find some happenings that could get me excited, hype, and happy. I read the letters my siblings and parents sent me.

One of the momentous and very memorable vacation times was when I was at the Rizal Memorial Park. On one beautiful afternoon at the Park, I was walking and relaxing when I met a beautiful girl. She doesn't seemed look like a city girl though, but she looks very pretty that I cannot resist my desire to talk to her. I said to myself, I have to find a way to talk to her.

I walked close to her and greeted her; "Hello, how are you? Nice day today and the Park, so, so beautiful and, and amazing." The girl was nice, accommodating, and very smart; "Yes it is. Is it your first time here?" I responded; "No, but I noticed they made some changes. They made it, it more beautiful. She said; "Yes they did." I nicely asked her; "You know the place. Do you, you live around here?" She responded with a smile; "No I live 5 miles away… it's about 3 miles east of the Park, in a big subdivision." I was amazed; "You, you must be very wealthy. Or, or the daughter of, of a rich man." She smile at me again; "No, I wish I am." I extended my hand and

142

introduced myself; "Boklit. My, my name is Boklit. What's yours?" "May, my name is May." I said; "You are living in a wealthy place…" She humbly said; "I know." I honestly told her I work in a night club. She just said; "Oh…"

May looked at me like she was wondering what I might have been doing in a night club- a dancer or a waiter or something else. I let her know right away; "I'm a Disc Jockey." May was not ashamed to tell me that she was just a domestic helper. I said to her; "You are so honest to tell me that…" She laughed and said; "Nothing to hide, you know." I was so surprised and said; "Wow! You could have hid it from me, you know what I mean? Some people bragged and…" But she said before I even finished my statement; "I don't really care." I said to her; "Me either.

You have a nice name." May said; "Thank you." "Boklit is, is not my real name." May was surprised to hear that, she thought I was making things up or lying to her. I made it clear to her; "It's just my, uhmm, my a-alias. People call me that since I, I was a little boy. I hope you're not upset." May casually said; "No I'm not, thanks and nice talking to you Boklit." She said that while turning her back from me. I responded with an invitation; "Nice to meet you and… can, can we see each other a-again? Can I buy you, you lunch or dinner someday?" May was hesitant when she said; "Ahh, uhhmm, that's a hard question. Why by the way?" We are both single, you know." May responded; "Alright. When and where?" Then she turned her back to walk away. I said; "Tomorrow." May stopped, turned her back to me and laughed out loud and said; "You're funny Boklit." I asked; "Why? What's fun-funny with what I said? Funny about what…?" She said; "I'm a maid, a domestic worker. Therefore Sundays or Saturdays off only, at least most of the time, for your info." I excitedly asked; "Does it mean o-okay?" She said; "No, not… It's not okay for tomorrow. May be…" I interrupted her; "Alright, next weekend." Sunday date came, I and May came out for dinner, and then we went out to watch a movie. We then decided to go to the Park where we first met.

At the Park, at Night with My Third Date

As we were walking at the Park, we were talking about our life, our experiences in the province where we came from, and our personal experiences at work. May asked me more of myself; "Tell me more about you Boklit." I honestly relate to her my life; "Night club was just a, a stepping for me, but looks like, like I am getting nowhere in there." May curiously asked; "Why?" I said; "I've wanted to, to be a, a professional singer, and my, my ex-girlfriend tried to helped me get to my dream, she helped me here in Manila. But…" I paused, but May insist; "What happened? So you have an ex…" I quickly responded; "Yes, my ex-girlfriend. We were decided to actually getting… we're set to get married already. We broke off because her, her parents and her boss and actually her uncle found out that we were seeing each other. Her studies were affected and, and because of our, our relationship, well you, you know they have to separate us. My girlfriend has to make a very hard decision. She has to, to side on her parents' decision all... although it both hurts us so much. It, it was beyond my, my control. They have to take her back to, to their province. I, I don't want to go back there, I don't hear from her..." I paused and I waited for her to make a comment.

I tried to control our conversation when I turned the conversation by asking her questions. "How about you May, tell me about you?" She smiled; "No boyfriend? I never have. I don't know." I aggressively said to her; "I just want to let you know that I'm able and I'm available." May has to go so she had to say good bye. "I have to say good bye for now." I said; "Same day, same time?" May said; "call."

At the Disco Club, Early in the Afternoon with Different Set Back that I Have to Overcome

The staff, the waiters, and all the workers were all working in preparations for the opening of the Gay Bar. I was at the booth cleaning up the messed inside the said booth. I picked up the garbage can to throw the garbage to the garbage bin. My fellow DJ (who was actually my senior) was at the door standing and smoking by the entrance of the Club talking with some guys. I looked at him like I was telling my fellow

DJ that I don't agree with him just standing there while everyone was busy.

The DJ asked sarcastically; "What's your problem? You have problem with me?" I sarcastically answered him; "I, I don't like it, you, you are a problem!" I dropped the rags and the garbage can and, with arrogance and anger, said to him, "I already cleaned up the booth and you're such, such a lazy person!" He was very mad, and he yelled at me; "So what!" I yelled back; "Well, nothing. I, I already have done your job!" He again sarcastically laugh at me; "Hahaha! It's your job, you are just an assistant." I yelled to this big man; "It's, it's, it's your job too!" He was trying to annoy me and made me mad; "That's part of your job too! Silly!" The cashier of the club and my friend tried to calm me down, but this guy was really into trouble. I did not know that he was on drugs at that time. Again, he sarcastically made fun of me when he said; "It's, it's, it's…" he laughed. He tried to mimic me. Again, he said; "That's, the, that's part of, of your job too!" I shouted; "That's part of your, your job too!" I swear and said something profane. He said; "I'm superior to you! I trained you!" and he cursed. I answer back; "It doesn't matter any, anymore!" I was even more outraged when he said; "You clean up the booth and I will play the music!"

I was eager to make him mad, I yelled at him; "You're lazy!" There, I got into his nerves, and he started to attack me and said; "I will punch you in your face if I hear you say that again!" I called him names and said to him; "Hey Big Man! Did you hear me say, say you, you are lazy! I then said something not nice to him and I yelled and cursing at him.

He was so furious and was really mad at me. There was a commotion between the two of us. I fell down on my face to the ground. I tried to get up, and I was having a hard time getting up. The security guard tried to help me and some of my friends helped me getting up. I was in violence again. I tried to lift up my face but I was so dizzy. He was coming to hit me again, but the security guard and some of my friends stopped him. I was beginning to recover while they were holding us and keeping us off from attacking each other. I ran to the kitchen and picked up the something to use to get even with him. Everyone thought I ran to go to our quarter. No one expected me to go to the kitchen to get something to execute violence. If you're hurt and blacked out, you will do anything to hit back. I quickly run out and attacked the DJ, but before I can even get near him; the manager and my best friend the supervisor in the club stopped and pinned me on the wall. They took care of me and made me relaxed and took out what was on my hand that may have caused harm to both of us. The manager asked me to calm down and he will let me go. I was still loud and really wanted to go after DJ but I can't get off. I looked at him like I wanted to eat him alive or beat him up to death.

I totally was blacked out in my thinking or in my mind that I did not know what was right and wrong. The manager whisper to my ear; "I'm going to let you go if you will be still and relaxed." I shouted; "Alright! Now, get, get your hands off me!" The manager said softly; "Ok, easy now." I got up and shrugged my shirt and pants, and looked around and swear to DJ and said; "I will not, not stop until I'm not finished with you." I made a death sign and gestures shouting to him; "You, you're done! You're done!" DJ; "I will just be here! Come and get me here!" I shouted; "I will!"

I left and I was followed by the manager as I took the taxi. The manager went back to where DJ was and started talking to him. The manager told him to go home because it was not safe for him to stay. They know I will come back to get him. He suggested; "You have to go home right now. It will not be safe for you. You know Boklit is so crazy and he meant what he said, especially you hurt him hard. If Boklit will come back, he might be back with his gang, and with revenge or gun." DJ; "Yes, but I still want my job." The manager promised him; "Yes I understand. Let me talk to the boss about this so he could discuss everything to Boklit and make him promise not to touch you or we will separate your shift of job."

In a Taxi at Night

It was around early of 1982. It was the years when Toyota Corolla and Toyota Corona as well as the Gemini were one of the famous Taxis in Manila and the provinces. Some of taxis were not even air conditioned. I was in that old taxi without an air conditioning since it was cheaper. It has radio but no tape recorder. Obviously, CD's were not even been in the minds of the inventors. The smog was not as bad as we have these days. I listened to the music of the Carpenters, the Cascades, Lettermen and Motown and other songs of the 70's on the radio of the taxi I was riding. Their music brought me back to my childhood from home up to where I was at that moment in time.

I reflect on the events when I was at the church with young people and Camps and Retreat we had. I remembered the songs and experiences I had at the church camp and retreat. I recalled the preaching of my brother also. While I was enjoying my taxi ride, I was reflecting and had flash back of my life in the province. I had a song in my mind and started singing it in my heart what my mother used to sing to me. Songs such as "Jesus I Come," "Jesus I Have Promised," and "What a Friend We Have in Jesus." I also imagined the time when I watched my dad and mom dancing from the music called 'Anniversary Song" our wealthy next door neighbor played every morning.

When I was in the hospital, my mother sang to me a hymn called "Jesus I Come." It was the same song I heard in our church when I was a young boy. I also remembered the member of the small church telling me that 'I could be a preacher someday like my brother' as she tapped me at my back. When I heard it, I talked to myself... I was mumbling; "It would be impossible. I'm just 10 years old, and it would take me 10 to 15 years to happen, and I don't think it would be possible." The lady at the church asked; "What did you say?" I said; "Nothing, I said I'm, I'm just a kid."

I went to my cousins and asked them to help me eliminate the DJ at that night club. He left after the incident. God did not let it happen or I may have end up in Federal prison and spend all my life there if we had killed him. Thankfully, he left and listened to our boss' advice to him.

I seek refuge and rest a while at my cousin's home. As far as I could remember, the place or compound where my cousin Ismael lives was the bulwarks of the largest cult in the Philippines. I literally entered another enemy's stronghold. In the dark street where I took off, I was met by a group of thugs. They were all on their way to where I was standing at that time. I was trying to figure out where the house of my cousin was. I was a little nervous of what the gangster may have in mind as they approached me. They were religious group of young people who were drinking at the alley. They stood around me without a word as I raised my hands and said; "I'm sorry, I, I'm here looking for my, my cousin." Thug: "We have a visitor, he lost his cousin." Everybody laugh at me. Thugs: "He lost his cousin, help him find his cousin!" Some of them may have thought of robbing me or may ask me to buy drinks for them as they would usually do. They will give you a shot or a bottle of beer and then they will ask for money to buy more drinks. I just looked at them and was so nervous because I can't handle them if they start the fight. They asked about my name. When I told them my name, they all laughed.

The thugs laughed louder this time. The neighbors started turning on their lights, some were peeping in their windows, while others opened their doors to check. I felt appeased when I saw some of the lights in the homes were turned on, and others opened their doors. They all were happy and we talked and I drink that night with the thugs and my cousin. I asked my cousin if I could get some help to finish up DJ. The gang agreed and they asked me his information, the time he comes in for work, and his facial appearance and heights. I and my cousin went back to the club but the DJ was not there anymore as I was told by some friends. They said he left and was so nervous that you might bring your gang here to finish him. I believe DJ and my boss had a tete a tete and it was about me.

He Finally Finished School!

My younger brother whom I supported in his seminary school has finally finished with academic honor. From then, he was giving me the spiritual advice. I was so happy and proud of him, but everything died down on me when he gave me the bad news. My enemy was coming, and he wanted to see me. Would you believe that? I did something bad on him and I betray his trust, and he was coming to my place to see me? He very well knew that I was crazy during those times due to my drug addiction and my issues at home, but why in the world is he going to come to my place. That was guts. I don't understand my parents and I don't understand my brother why they gave him my address in Manila. When they told me the news, I assumed that he was coming to execute his revenge on me at the night club. I was not afraid of him, I just don't want to hurt him anymore or kill him this time because I was suspicious of him already. I believe everyone will agree with my feelings and (perhaps) false assumption.

I warned my buddies about him and warned them of his possible risk back; you know his revenge on me for what I did to him years back. But I told them not to hurt him, and to just hold him and scare him or just warn him of what may happen to him if he hurt me. You know, hiding in Luzon or in Metro Manila if you're wanted by the Law is not a bad idea because Luzon and Manila is huge. That's what I thought why he was eager to come to my place and see me.

Tete a Tete with My Boss

My boss talked to me about what happened with me and DJ and told me about their personal conversation at the office. He talked to DJ about what we would do, and the boss has agreed that he will separate us. My boss said; "Please don't do anything stupid. I will see you both tonight okay?" While I was still dealing with my recent enemy, I am dealing with my former enemy at the same time. It did not take long; the guy came and inquired of me. He was ushered to where I was. Of course everyone knows that they will not let me be in trouble with anyone. We talked, and I was surprised that the only reason he came was to ask for help because he was applying for a job in Manila as a new college graduate.

I apologized to him for what I did to him in Bacolod City, and apology was accepted, and I was happy. He said; "Forget about it, I told my parents and your parents that I forgave you already. They were all against my idea, because they said you're crazy. "Sorry." I laughed. "They were right." We both laughed. I said, "Thanks, man." He said comfortably; "I don't see any danger seeing you again." I said to him; "I'm trying to be… I, I tried but every time I try, try to be… I don't know something crazy will, will happen." He asked; "You want to change but…?" I said; "Yes, I wanted to be good be… because I'm having a miserable life here, and, and I'm scared to die." We talked for few hours then he asked to leave. "Well I have to go, and it's good you're thinking of change. You can and you try to go back to school. Stay away from trouble my friend." I responded nicely; "I'll, I will, and these are all in, in me. I mean your bills. Thanks for stopping by… and, I'm so sorry." He just gave me a smile, a thumb up and a hug. Then he left, giving me the most comfortable feeling I had in my lifetime during my times in the Disco Club.

The Force and Power Within Me That I Can't Overcome

I was in a restaurant just by myself. It was the first time I was drunk and just by myself. It was also one of the happiest times in my life in the Disco Club. I ordered food, so much food like I was celebrating something special. The waitress was wondering if I was waiting for someone to join me. I kept on drinking and did not bother how much

I already consumed. I left that restaurant drunk and went to another restaurant just to sit and play the Juke Box. The couple in that restaurant across my work place was having breakfast. The gentleman was having a good time playing music at the Juke Box.

After a while, the man went to the restroom. The woman was left alone at the table. I chat with her and we were seen by her boyfriend talking. She was a dancer at the club next door. The guy was jealous and we started to dislike each other by showing through our gestures. I looked at him like I was trying to annoy him and seduced him to hate me. I went to the Juke Box and played the music she really wanted to dance with at the Night Club. The man was jealous and furious at me. He got mad, I got mad. I grabbed him in his chest and punched him on solar plexus. He was hurt, and I picked him up and put my face on his face, and said; "You see this face? You remember this face if you're in my territory. I don't care who you are, you respect this face." I then let him go, and they left.

I never knew that he reported me to his gang and they set me up. The guy and his girlfriend called me out because they said they wanted to settle the issue and apologize. I did not bother granting his request; therefore, I went out. But when I was out already, there were other guys hiding by the side of the restaurant. As soon as I was out, they started beating me up. I was alone and there were a couple of them, so I ran across the street in the Pub where I was working, and grabbed the bolo. I put it in a native bag made of coconut leaves. I pursued after them not knowing that they were all ready to kill me.

They had all kinds of weapons. Iron Pipe, chains,

wooden bar, belt, and knives. When I got closed to the Disco Club where they were working; I was set up already. I felt two people were holding my hands and told me not to move. Someone took my native bag and bolo. I was hit from behind while I can't move because I was locked up by their hands. I saw the couple was coming out of the door while the lady was crying and pleading for his boyfriend to stop and just let go. She tried to stop her boyfriend from killing me by stabbing me with the kitchen knife. When he was about to stab me, his girlfriend embrace me and said; "If you kill him, you have to kill me first." That gave me the time to move and run. But just a few meters was another group waiting. I was beat up like I was a basketball being passed around by punch and kick, and with belt and stick. I thought I was going to get killed by beatings. Then someone hit me with iron pipe at the back of my head, and I felt down on my knees, then I shouted; "Oh My...!" It was the only words I know in my desperate situation in calling God for help. It was the shortest prayer I ever prayed in a life and death situation. As soon as I shouted those words, I saw them running away. I fell down and lost consciousness for a while.

After a while I got up and tried to get home to our quarters in the club; and right at the door I fell down trying to get in. The cashier of the Disco Club was awakened by the bang of my head on the door. He helped me and woke everyone up. It was about 9:00 to10:00 in the morning. As night club employees, we worked grave shift and sleep on day time. My friend called the cops and they took me to the hospital. The sweater that I bought the day before was tore off like it was unrecognizable already. That was I believe the turning point of my life.

My Lowest Point in Life Just Got Started

It was the lowest point in my life. I was really so discouraged and I thought I was going to get back to this man and his gang and won't mind spending my life in jail. I felt like everything in my past was erased in an instant, and I was walking in a new mission and new goals of doing something worst than I wanted since I was a boy with the knowledge of what is right and wrong or in my years of accountability.

Few days after the incident, a group of men who looked like military men were looking for me. My supervisor called me from our quarter and asked me to come with him. He ushered me to these 3 men who I believed were demolition or salvage team. I called them "Demolition Team" or "Salvage Team" as the police and military term during those times where they were in charge of picking up the suspect and kill them and throw their bodies to the swamp. The Filipino term was you will be picked up at the swamp, or in 'kangkongan' (kang- kong-an) 'Species of edible plant that grows in a swamp'. They offered me 2 things: 1- They wanted me to join their team. 2- They wanted me to pinpoint the people who beat me up. I was speechless because my mind was travelling a hundred miles per hour, thinking of so many things in a flash of time. I was wondering- how in the world they knew me and my name when I never even met them in my whole life? How did they know I was beat up few days back? Why do they want me to join their team? What kind of job was it? I actually asked them the kind of job they were offering me. Why are they interested on the people who hurt me? I passed the offer and went back to our quarter.

It became a time of reflection for me although I did not know the term for it, but I did. It was during my very depressive moment in life. But I believe it was already the Holy Spirit working in me without my knowledge because I was in the dark side of the world.

I Was so Depressed When I Heard Those Words

It should have been the good news for me because there were people who wanted to take the revenge for me and put the matter in their hands; but it made me so depressed, and gave me more miseries, and questions. I walked from the door of our quarter to my bed, and stood up, I then walked back and forth like a restless person with no direction and purpose. I really felt miserable and hopeless. I was so sad and lonely, and I was clueless of what to do next. I can feel that there is something missing in my life, and I can sense an emptiness that I've never felt before. I was so overwhelmed by the bad times and bad things I was going through. I sat down and was stilled, looking around, looking at the picture of my ex-girlfriend. No one's at the quarter that night, everyone was at work in the club. The noise of the music at the club and my heart, which was longing, were battling over control.

There was a knocked at the door. I looked at the door and was hesitant to open it. I slowly walked towards the door, still feeling dizzy and hurting so much both physically, emotionally, and the spiritual longing that obviously was there. I touched the door knob and asked; "Who is it?" It was the manager of the club. She asked me; "Boklit, we have some gentlemen here that were sent by the boss, and they need to talk to you. They are here to talk to you and help you." I opened the door, I let the gentlemen comes in and offered them a seat. They were the secret agents in Manila, and they were my boss's friends. When they came to investigate and asked for the details of the people involved, I was straightforward and provided them information. I told them they were from across the street working in the other club. They wanted me to work with them and to cooperate with them. They really wanted for me to help them solve my issues with these guys who became wanted by the law. I asked them; "Can you just, just leave me alone for now. You know that I, I, I'm hurting and I'm in pain. I just want to be alone and, and just be, be by, by myself." Everyone was quiet. They looked at each other, and signalled to go.

The manager talked to me and she said; "Boklit, we will let you rest and have your time. But I want you to cooperate with them once you're able to communicate well, and feeling better. The boss and them agreed to work hard to get your enemies or whatever and whoever is involved. You have their phone numbers to call, you know what to do."

They all left. As soon as they closed the door, I took a deep breath, sat down, and covered my face. When I lift up my head and saw a white envelope. My curiosity drove me to pick up such and opened the letter. It was actually an official envelope with red, white, and blue printed on each side. I stood up, and curiously checked where it was from, and to whom it was sent. It was from Bacolod City. It was a letter sent to me by my brother. I opened the white envelope and read it. I tried to check all the verses in the Bible, but I don't know how to open it or check the books, chapters and verses. I felt like a fool and crazy having no idea of the things of God. I pray instead. I had a flash back again of the Indian street preacher in Bacolod Plaza preaching about salvation and the Lord's coming.

I stood still… I grabbed all my stuff and put them in plastic bag and small old luggage. I also picked up the green New Testament Bible my brother sent me and got out of the room in the middle of the night. I overheard the music from the Disco Club, but when I opened the door; it was so loud and I can hear the voices of the people in the Disco House. I heard the DJ say something. The waiters, the staff and everyone in the night club were all busy working. Everyone was loud, happy, and some were counting their tips. As I opened the door, it caught everybody's attention, including my boss who was at the time counting part of the money the club made for the night.

Everyone slowly stopped talking and ceased from what they were doing at the moment. I stood still at the door, looked at everybody, and I walked slowly towards the boss. The boss asked; "What's up Boklit?" I dropped my plastic bag and luggage and said; "Boss, I, I need to go. My boss asked me curiously; "Where are you going?" I said; "I am quitting my job." My boss asked; "Why? You don't like the pay, or you don't like what you're doing?" I answered respectfully; "None, none of those, I mean, it's not, it's not it." Again he asked; "Why and what are your reasons for quitting your job?" As he continued counting the money and writing on something. I said; "No boss, not about that, not about money or… I just want to start a new life, or, or something new." The boss stopped what he was doing and looked at me with surprise and curiosity and said; "New life? What do you mean of New Life?" I said; "I don't real, really know, I, I just want to get out of this place, and, and do something else… like, I don't know." My boss was so understanding and helpful. "Alright, I will let you go. Here's some cash and be good this time. Have a good trip, and take care. You are always welcome to come back any time."

The boss looked at me and shook his head. He can't believe I was leaving just like that. But in spite of my random and hasty or quick decisions, he was still gracious to me that he even offered me to come back any time I want, and they'll still have the job open for me. He said you will still have a job in the club and still welcome at the club anytime you come back. I thanked him and everybody gave me a hug, some gave me some cash, others a hand shake, and some of the ladies gave me a kissed. It was a very emotional morning for everybody. They all stopped what they were doing and followed me on my way out. The security guard hugged me, and DJ approached me and shook my hand. They all stayed outside of the Disco Club until I hopped in the cab. Some of them were in tears as they wave good bye to me especially the boy that I helped when he was bullied by the security guard. He waved back and the taxi left. I went to the bus station to go to my brother who is a pastor of the Southern Baptist Church in Baguio City.

Getting Out of the Old Place to a New Place

While I was in the bus, I was thinking of my life in the past, and what I should do next. I was in the bus travelling to Baguio City with no concrete plans and focus or direction in terms of my future. I was going to my brother hoping to try to get enrolled and get some education, and I did not know what course to take if accepted. I arrived in Baguio and met my oldest brother. We hugged and we were happy to see each other after a long time of absence. We started talking about our life. I just turned 22 years old at that time.

I started talking to my brother about our father abuses and his drunkenness. My brother who was a pastor of the Southern Baptist Church in Baguio City counselled me and made me understand my father. It was because of my dad's family background and his bad life and family frustrations. He said; "Our father and mother used to be wealthy before the war. Our grandfather has a business and properties. Our grandparents has Spanish heritage. They were wealthy as well. They all lost their wealth during World War II. The frustrations of dad due to the losses, including our first 2 eldest siblings adds up to his problems in dealing with himself, with his family, and the environment that he lives in. Our father did not have formal education too, and that made it harder for him to accept. All these were because of war and things that happened which are all beyond his control."

My brother also explained to me the psychological part of why our father was doing what he was doing. My brother again explained to me everything to make me understand my dad; "Our father is smart, he was just a victim of circumstances and it dawned on him. He was very disciplinarian, very strict because he doesn't want us to be like him- a failure. He want to see us live a good life and with education. He wants to keep us away from the life we have right now. He uses 'reverse psychology' but he did not know how to make it work for us. He just can't, or because father do not know how to execute it properly or in a right way. Father is just like any other father who desires the best for their children. Most of the times the reverse psychology that he was doing to us were not properly said and done in a way that we can picked it up because of father's lacked of formal education. I hope he will really know God in a very personal way where he could be humble enough to accept his weaknesses and all his mistakes."

I interrupted my brother and asked him while we have a jeepney ride going to the market then to the seminary. I said; "Alright, I got it. Can, can I study here?" My brother asked me; "Do you have college degree?" I ashamedly answered; "Not even high school." He was surprised; "What? What did you finish?" I said; "Third year high school in five High Schools. I was in fourth year (12 grade) but did not graduate". He repeated my answer; "Third year high school in five high schools? How did...?" I explained; "I went to five High Schools and I did not finished 4th year because of lacked of attendance and, and I transferred too much." My brother sadly said, "This is not the place for you." I thought I can go back to school in Baguio City, but I can't be qualified to get enrolled as what my brother told me. I failed in my first goal to accomplish.

I Left Baguio City to Explore in My Cousin's Place in Malabon, Metro Manila

I remember getting off from the bus from the Summer Capital of the Philippines to the Flood Capital of the Philippines. I got off the bus, and I can already smell the aroma. In Baguio City- It was from the aroma of pine trees, flowers, fresh vegetables and fresh fruits. In Malabon- it was the aroma of junk, dirty water and stagnant water of the rivers, fish, and dried fish, and the smell of the fish sauce and factories. The dirt from the ocean that goes back to the creeks, and small rivers, and other unpleasant environment was something really new to me. We had a nice place in the club compared to where I was in at that time of which I could say, 'I was homeless'. I heard the cock crow, the dogs barking, and it was very dark.

I was looking at a piece of paper with the name and address of my cousin Ismael. After checking on few houses, I finally found the address. It was just a room, a very small room in a slum area. It was not even a studio type or far from being like a studio type. I was reminded of our home in the province, in Bacolod City. I knocked on the door of the house of Ismael. I called; "Ismael! Ismael! Ismael! No one answered. The neighborhood checked on me. I tried knocking and calling on Ismael again. I was persistent and kept on trying. Finally Ismael woke up and open the door to check. Ismael queried; "Who is it?" I said; "Ismael, it's me, Boklit." Ismael let me in. I told him I lost my job, and I have nowhere to go. I asked him if I could stay there for a while until I can find a job. He graciously agreed. Ismael at that time was living by himself in an 8 by 12 square foot room the way I figured out the size of the room. Everything was in that small room.

I also wondered why almost everything was hanging by the wall so I asked. He said that on high tide because he lived close to the ocean; the water rises about an inch or two below his bed we called 'Papag' or 'Flat bed made of plywood'. It was funny and very interesting because on Summer time, we don't feel the heat of the summer because we felt like we were always sitting and sleeping in water bed. Yes, the bed was also our chair and table. If you forgot to hang your sandal when its high tide, you will start swimming to get hold of your sandals or you can replace such with the new one that will float around the small room or outside the house.

We had free aquarium, free water to wash our feet, and free pool if we were not really meticulous of the dirt and smell of the water. Sometimes, I felt like I was eating by the side of the pool or sea shore. All that changed from all concrete room to a sandy, watery, and smelly room. I appreciate my cousin Ismael for letting me stay there. I was not complaining. I am just trying to give everyone a good picture of how my life changed overnight.

My First Meal in My New Home and New Horizon

My first meal as I started my new life and new environment with my cousin Ismael in his house in Malabon. Ismael prepared a meal for me and asked me to grab some plate and make some coffee for the two of us. I suggested he could go back to bed I will take care of myself. He agreed because he had to work later in the day at the auto repair shop. I ate my breakfast and drink my coffee while checking on the magazine of the religious cults in the Philippines founded by a Filipino. Later that day, while Ismael was away, I read the New Testament from the book of Psalms 23. I also read Romans chapter eight. These are the verses that really hit me, and I felt the presence of God right there.

> *The Bible says "There is therefore now no condemnation to them which are in Christ Jesus, who walk not after the flesh, but after*

the Spirit. 2 *For the law of the Spirit of life in Christ Jesus hath made me free from the law of sin and death. 3 For what the law could not do, in that it was weak through the flesh, God sending his own Son in the likeness of sinful flesh, and for sin, condemned sin in the flesh: 4 That the righteousness of the law might be fulfilled in us, who walk not after the flesh, but after the Spirit. 5 For they that are after the flesh do mind the things of the flesh; but they that are after the Spirit the things of the Spirit. 6 For to be carnally minded is death; but to be spiritually minded is life and peace. 7 Because the carnal mind is enmity against God: for it is not subject to the law of God, neither indeed can be. 8 So then they that are in the flesh cannot please God. 9 But ye are not in the flesh, but in the Spirit, if so be that the Spirit of God dwell in you. Now if any man have not the Spirit of Christ, he is none of his. 10 And if Christ be in you, the body is dead because of sin; but the Spirit is life because of righteousness. 11 But if the Spirit of him that raised up Jesus from the dead dwell in you, he that raised up Christ from the dead shall also quicken your mortal bodies by his Spirit that dwelleth in you. 12 Therefore, brethren, we are debtors, not to the flesh, to live after the flesh. 13 For if ye live after the flesh, ye shall die: but if ye through the Spirit do mortify the deeds of the body, ye shall live. 14 For as many as are led by the Spirit of God, they are the sons of God. 15 For ye have not received the spirit of bondage again to fear; but ye have received the Spirit of adoption, whereby we cry, Abba, Father. 16 The Spirit itself beareth witness with our spirit, that we are the children of God: 17 And if children, then heirs; heirs of God, and joint-heirs with Christ; if so be that we suffer with him, that we may be also glorified together. 18 For I reckon that the sufferings of this present time are not worthy to be compared with the glory which shall be revealed in us." (Romans 8:1- 18 KJV)*

I stopped right there in verse 18 and started reading from the top and really tried to understand it. I was convinced that Apostle Paul talks about sin but I was not convicted or repentant yet. I love it when I was on verses fourteen to eighteen. I have so much interest on the Bible. It also strikes my heart when I read about the promised of God in the midst of our sufferings here on earth. I was also interested to know on the promised of eternal life, and the promised of being God's heirs- heirs of God in Christ.

Ismael came home later in the afternoon, and he noticed that I was reading my Bible. Ismael inquired, "When did you start reading the Bible? I thought you lost interest with God and the Bible since we left the province?" I said; "You know that, that my brother Samson all, always made me read on Sat, Saturdays. That's why, I, I hated Saturdays when I was a little boy." He asked; "Then you turned yourself from God. I said; "No, I don't have God. I just placed God in, in my pockets and dreams. I was all, always thinking of money and, and going to Japan to perform, and, and be famous." Ismael recalled to me about my drug problem; "I heard about you being wanted in Bacolod, and your drug problems and..." I quickly answered; "I know. I ran away from home. Father... and I..." I paused... "I don't want to talk about it now, you know him. He is like your father but mine is worst." Ismael quip about my scars on my face and head. "Yea, by the way, what happened to your face and head?" I tried to change the topic of our conversation. I asked him about his job, his siblings who lives nearby, and his family back home.

Ismael was persistent to know about my scars by keeping on asking me the same question. I finally told him firmly to not worry about it. Then I asked him about church; "Do, do you go to church?" Ismael excitedly answered; "Yea, I go to true church. My older brother is one of the leaders there." I said; "Good, great, I, I like that... and" Ismael interrupted me and said; "Beautiful girls too. They come here to pick me up for church." I had a slight changed on my facial expression from being happy, excited and positive to wondering and frowning facial reactions of why would he go to church for the girls that he likes? Again he said; "Beautiful girls? They pick me up for church? We come together." He noticed my disagreement and asked me; "Is there something wrong with what I said?" I replied, "No, I'm just wondering what, what kind of church it is." He mentioned to me the church which is one of the largest cults in the Philippines.

Ismael wanted to capitalize my situation, when he said to me; "You know those beautiful girls. You are homeless they can help and give you a job." I started thinking, walking back and forth. I was deeply worried of what Ismael said. Ismael just watched me being so uneasy in our small room. He asked; "What's wrong? What's in your mind? Why are you…?" I excitedly said; "Wait! I was thinking… How about this; I will give you, you choices- first, you will come with me to, to that church at the corner. You know, the one that is just a, a block away from here. Then the, the following Sunday, I, I will go to the church with you, the one you are talking about… then I, I can figure out, I mean we… you know. We can know which church we should belong."

I made the proposal to Ismael because I wanted to go to a Baptist church, but I don't want to disappoint Ismael. I also made a deal with Ismael, because I wanted to stay away from his church. I believe it was not the right church that he was looking for.

He proposed; "But the church at the corner; they don't have a good building, and no beautiful girls to pick you up. Come to this church and I will do my best to get you a job." I said; "I don't care, I, I want a church like the one in Bacolod City you know, that, that little Baptist church. I remember the camps, the, the fellowships, the outings, the fun, the retreats, and, and the crushes we have there too… hahaha… I laughed so hard." We both laughed out loud. Ismael recalled; "You remember your fist fight with that professional singer, you know he sounds like Matt Moron." I corrected him; "Not Matt Moron, It's Matt Monro. I know, at the church- a fist fight." I shook my head in disbelief of what I did at church when I was a teenager. I looked at Ismael and said this; "Sometimes,

I can't even be… I can't believe, I, I had a fist fight with this guy at church."

Then Came Sunday

I asked Ismael if he could come with me to the Baptist church or take me there before he goes to his church. I also made a proposal to him that if he will come with me on Easter to the Baptist church nearby, I will come to his church the following Sunday, and he agreed. It was Easter Sunday. It was my first Sunday in that place and my first Sunday in a Baptist church for a long time. It was April 11, 1982 when we first came to visit this Baptist church. I got up early in the morning for the first time in a very long time. I dressed up and was ready for church before Ismael got up that morning. We went to church that day. As we enter the church, we were greeted by the ushers and seated us on the pews. During that Sunday, the church speaker was Estus Pirkle. He was the producer on the movie that we watched that night. We did not know, neither had any idea of his visit, and that he was one of the actor on that movie. Neither did we ever know about the movie, but we were there to just be at church.

We sat about four rows back because we were shy, and we did not know anyone from that church, therefore we were thinking sitting at the back will make us more comfortable. It was expected of a pastor to preach about resurrection on Easter Sunday, and sure enough he did.

But every time he preached and talked about sin, hope, salvation, misery, and repentance, I felt like he was pointing his finger on me and directly talking about me. I felt like he knew me and he knew what I was doing in the night club. At the end of his preaching, he extended an invitation for everyone to come to accept the Lord. I was a very shy person, but that day, I did not care about the people around me and what they will say about me. I slowly took my first step to come forward to accept the Lord, but I felt like I was running forward already.

It was an 11:00 a.m. worship service dated April 11, 1982 at International Baptist Church- Malabon, and at that time the church were fully packed since it was Easter Sunday. This day became more significant to me not only that that was the day I was born again, but my only daughter was born on the same date ten years after my conversion.

I felt like I got to the front in a split of a second. I was crying like never had before. I cried like a baby as Reverend Eddie Banquillo was counselling me. The Lord at that time was like pointing to me one by one the sins that I committed in the night club and when I was back home in Bacolod City. Pastor Eddie explained to me again the message that I heard from my childhood in the Sunday school class at the church I grew up in, and in their extension in our area. Who can forget the Indian street preacher who was preaching the same message in Bacolod plaza? Absolutely, my brother Ephraim's letter to me has the same message as well.

I never had a feeling like what I felt after I surrendered my life to God. It was the very first time in my life that I felt like something just got out of my mind, of my heart, and my whole being. There was something that just filled me with something that I can't even explain. I felt light and peaceful. It was something I never felt before.

I witnessed to an old gentleman at the hospital few years ago while I was there confined for some stomach pain. A Christian friend of mine who was working at the said hospital found out that I was there for treatment came to visit me and shared to me about a man who was scared of death and eternal punishment to those who reject God. She recommended me to this patient who needs help and needed to get over his fear and other emotional and spiritual problems he had. They transported this man from other floor to my room so I could start talking to him about God and the resolution to his fear. I shared to him the gospel and how he could overcome his fear and anxiety. He accepted the Lord and was willing to let go of everything in his life and mind. After we prayed he said; "I felt like all the rats in my mind just came out, and I felt peace…" I shared this story because that was I felt when I accepted the Lord that day.

We came home with happiness, and we both enjoyed our time together at church. Ismael likes the church, and he likes the young people and especially the girls our age. It was maybe because we were visitors, and it was expected of them to be nice to us. We felt welcomed, accepted, and we also felt the Spirit of love and care from our fellow young people. It was one of the amazing moments in life I had since I left the night club. I can feel that my life since I quit my job was beginning to be more on track and directive as compared to when I was out with the wrong people and in a wrong place. The following few days, we were visited by the church's Christian workers. Ismael and I had a brief Bible Study with them in Ismael's small room. I appreciate what they did because they rolled up their pants and took off their shoes so they can cross the usual high tide flood in our place to visit us.

Ismael and I were looking forward for the Sunday following after that visit in a Baptist church. Will it be at the same church the coming Sunday or the Cult's congregation? It was the day we look forward into. The big Sunday for Ismael where I believe he was looking forward for us to come and visit the Cults congregation where he belong to as a member, but I have something different in mind. When that Sunday came, I woke up, and to my surprise, Ismael was fully ready to go to church. He was dressed up and already had set up the breakfast for the two of us. I was thinking of the promise I had for him- we will go to their church. I was thinking Ismael was really excited to see me in his church, and to see those beautiful girls. After breakfast, we left for church; however, we encountered problem along the way.

We Were Blocked from Coming to a Baptist Church

Ismael was so happy that day as we both walked our way to the church. Unfortunately, there was problem along the way. We were blocked in the alley by a group of young men from the said cults' group. They asked us where we were going and we told them to church. I wondered why Ismael did not tell them to go to their church. They ridiculed us and told me that I am homeless and jobless. They said that the Baptist church can't help me and will not help me. They said that the Baptist will just take our money and would not care about us. They promised me that if I will go to their church, they will give me a new job, and help me find a room to rent. They even promised me to introduce me to the girls in their congregation. I told them that I was not coming to that church for a job or something, but to worship. We asked them if they could let us go and pass the alley, and they did. We walked through the alley to take a jeepney or tricycle. I tried to cross the road to catch a jeepney or a tricycle to church where Ismael goes, but he just keep on walking on a different direction. I stopped and asked him; "Where are you going?" He answered, "We're going to the Baptist church!" I was so happy and excited that he decided to go back. Ismael accepted the Lord as well, and he never went back to his former religion. He became very much involve until now to that same church.

I Was Homeless and Jobless, but Not Hopeless

It's not easy to live in someone else's home especially if you don't have a job. Although I did not have a job and I was homeless;

at least during those times that I was going through those pain and suffering in life, I don't feel hopeless unlike when I was in the province and the night club. But hope was there. One Sunday the pastor was announcing about the Bible College that the church is supporting, and of which the pastor of the church was the dean of the seminary. He announced that anyone who would want to get enrolled in the seminary will receive a free board and lodging, free education, and a small amount of financial support. I was seated at the back of the church and I said to Ismael; "This is what I need and what I have been looking for." Ismael asked; "What do you mean?" I whisper to him; "You hear what he said; "Free dormitory, free food, free education, and a little financial support. You see, I'm homeless, I need to eat, I wanted to get an education, and I need money. All that I need were there already." Therefore, the truth is I did not enrolled the seminary because God spoke to me to go there and be a preacher. I send myself there because I have nowhere to go, and I don't have the ability to support myself to get formal education, and other necessities. I came to know the Lord as my Savior on April 11, 1982, and enrolled at the seminary on June of the same year. It means that I was only about 2 months in my Christian life.

Did I just use those opportunities? I don't believe so. I believe God used the opportunity so He can take me where He wanted me to be. I was rebellious and hard headed. He has to take all that I have so He can give me what He has planned for me. I went to the seminary with marijuana and records of rock music in my bags. I still listen to rock music while I was in the seminary and I did not surrender my marijuana, not until I heard the preacher named Major Cruz who preached about witch craft and other sins that enslaved us. I came forward to surrender to God my slavery to many sins and I asked God to washed me and free me by the power of the blood of the Lamb and in the name of Jesus.

> *"Proverbs 4:3 KJV For I was my father's son, tender and only beloved in the sight of my mother." Fathers have a special place in the hearts and minds of children. You may have heard them (the children) bragged and talked of their father's love, counsels, accomplishments, and wisdom... Here in this verse and the whole chapter- it tells us of the father's heart and mind. Read the whole chapter to see the real picture. "Proverbs 4:4 KJV He taught me also, and said unto me, Let thine heart retain my words: keep my commandments, and live." The Bible says; "Proverbs 4:20 KJV My son, attend to my words; incline thine ear unto my sayings. Proverbs 7:2 KJV Keep my commandments, and live; and my law as the apple of thine eye."*

My Dad's Health Deteriorated, and He was Dying

Because of my dad's abused on his health, he was sick and weak. It was about that year 1982 when I heard about the death of my grandmother and my dad's health's deterioration. During those times, my mom was in and out of the hospital, too, because of acute ulcer, and acute arthritis. My grandmother passed away while all these problems were piling up. The devil was attacking in a different way this time. I've forgiven my dad when I became a Christian. I even wrote them a letter that I got saved, and I was going to enter the Seminary. I asked for their advice and approval as well. Yes, I was devastated when he was sick and when my mom got sick as well. I was hurt when my grandmother passed away but I was happy to hear from my mother, my sister and siblings that grandmother came to know the Lord as well.

I was pastor of a church in Subic when my dad shared this story to me. It was on the early nineties when they were with us for vacation. One day at church while I was seated outside the church enjoying the sunset, my dad sat next to me. He said he wanted to share his story to me. I asked him what story. He shared to me his experienced that day when he was very sick. He said the doctor and the medical examiner declared him dead already when he was at the hospital. But he came back to life. He said he died and saw his body while the real him was departing and went to heaven.

Ely Roque Sagansay

He said when he died he literally went up to heaven and saw heaven and God in His throne. He can't see the face of God because it was so bright that he can't even look at. As he bowed down before the throne of God, he said that God told him to go back to earth because He is not done with him yet. My dad came back to life and came to know the Lord as His Savior and Lord. It was almost the same year that I came to know the Lord. From that time on, my dad was never been the same. It was the unexpected day of salvation and conversion of my dad.

My dad became so faithful in the work of the Lord. God changed him. He never went back to his old life. My friend Noly Bustamante who once visited our home in Bacolod City asked me one day where my dad was working, why he would leave at 6:00 AM and come home at 6 to 8:00 PM. My friend can't believe that dad goes to church every day to help the pastor and to serve. The Lord used him mightily in the church's work and ministry. My dad became a lighthouse and a testimony of His grace in our community and village. He became the pastor's second man.

I Went Back to the Disco Club

After several weeks that I got saved, I asked my pastor Dr. Pio S. Tica if I could go back to the club where I used to work. He refused to let me go, but I insist because I wanted to share to my friends the Word of God. After my conversion, I had

178

my very long hair cut, I shaved and wear a little formal clothes. I went to the club in the afternoon just about time they got up or just had lunch.

When I came in inside the club, everyone was curiously looking at me. They did not recognize me obviously. When I was closed to where they were at and I started talking, they were surprised to see me. They asked me questions such as; "What happened to me, why I had my hair cut?" Why did I shave my beard and mustache and why I looked so formal and decent?" I told them about my salvation experienced, and about the Lord and how to be saved and be forgiven of our sins. Guess what happened, I went back home so discouraged. They all laughed at me like they don't know me or care if I once a violent, drug addict, and trouble maker man. I went there to witness to them, but I became a laughing stock to them. They started making fun of me and I was like nothing to them, that I decided to leave early. I was sad and hurt as a new believer.

I Found the Girl I Am Going Marry

One Sunday my cousin and I decided to sit outside the church for a change. It was the first time I really stared at Vemerlyn Dumala the whole time that she was at the stage singing with her Ensemble. There were eight of them in the team. The Green light Ensemble was singing so beautifully but I had my attention and eyes on the beautiful lady in the

middle. I looked at her like she was Mary the mother of
the Lord Jesus Christ in the flesh. I told Ismael; "You see
that beautiful girl in the middle with curly hair?" Ismael
asked; "Yes, what about her?" I confidently said; "That
girl will be my wife someday." Ismael laughed at me and
looked at me with kind of doubt or insult or disagreement
and said; "She will not like you and she will not talk to
you. Look at her; she is a Bible woman and look at you!"
I was so mad at Ismael that I confronted him when we
got home. I did not care already if I lost my privilege of
staying in his small room.

*The very first time I saw her I said to myself- this is the girl
that I'm going to marry someday.* I made a covenant to God
right there while I was looking at her singing during the
worship service. I said to God; "Lord, if you will give her
to me as my girlfriend, I promised you, I am going to
respect her. I will not kiss her, not until we are at the altar
on our Wedding Day. I will not hurt her or do something
similar to what I did to the girls who trusted me and
shared their love to me. I will try to be a good boyfriend
and husband to her."

During those times, the church was under construction.
There were stones, pebbles and rocks everywhere and so
dusty. I told Ismael that I'm going to talk to her after the
worship service. Fresh from the night club and I still have
those fresh feeling and attitude of a man with unbelievers'
mind set and rough approach to ladies. During that day, I
was wearing jeans and a high boots with high heels, and a
plain t-shirt. I looked like a hippie with long hair.

After the service, I went straight to the front to catch
her before she goes to the ladies dormitory of the church.

I was in a hurry. But when Vemerlyn saw me coming, she started to run away from me like she saw a monster. I shouted, "Hey! I just want to know your name!" She ran fast as she could with her sister Evelyn. I tried to run after them, but just a few steps from the church building, the heel of my boots break off, and I started running like a lame man. I looked back, and I saw the heel of my boots was behind me. I went back walking to pick up the heel. It was very embarrassing and I saw Ismael and other people looking at me were all laughing at me. I went by the side of the church smashing my shoes on the wall of the church building trying to fix it with a big stone. It was funny but that was the start of my true 'Love Story'. Do you think it's a good idea to write what happened next?

~Fin~

Uncut Interview of Director Vic Tiro with My Brothers

My name is Ephraim, and I'm the 10th among the siblings. I was called "Gamay," which means small or least. Most of my siblings are sports minded, and they are always in the forefront, and I always stayed at home. There were four of us that were little and Ely is the oldest among the last four siblings. Then, we have one girl whose name is Aidariza. We were all together in almost everything while we were growing up. We were very close since we only have one bed in our room, and we all sleep there together.

I remember that we cannot even put ourselves together in one mosquito net and in one big blanket. I remember that when those days when they go out to watch the movie, I would be at home just by myself. I have never watched a movie with them. They enjoyed the movie, and I can't because I would definitely have some bed bug bites when we get home coming from the theater. When they get home, they brought with them the bed bugs from the theater.

Pastor Ely had done a lot of good things and a lot of bad things at the same time. I remember when I would ask for bread from him, and he would spit on his bread. So instead of you wanting to eat some of his bread, you would decide not to do it anymore, and that's one of his jokes and humor I can't forget about him. That's just one of his gags that he was doing in our house. He was always out there doing something and I would be staying at home by myself. He could have the good fortune if he went in schooling. But he went to so many schools, I think in four high schools as far as I could remember. He went into 3rd year high school, and he already had four schools… From you know, Domingo Lacson High School, then, to Bacolod City High School, and then in NIT (Negros Institute and Technology, and night school at Negros Occidental High School. He also went to Guimaras in IloIlo at Good Shepherd Fold Academy, and he became a problem to them there, too. He didn't get to finish school because he enjoys playing tennis and making money at the tennis court.

I observed earlier when I was studying at the Rizal Elementary School, I see him in the Bacolod plaza selling newspapers, does shine shoes, selling sweepstakes, paper bags and other things making money. He did that from elementary to third year high school. He will come from Rizal Elementary School to the Bacolod plaza doing all those things. When we passed by the plaza, no one will touch us because he is famous in the Bacolod City plaza and respected by the bystanders our age.

During his childhood, he did a lot of stupid things and one of them is that there is no week or month that some neighbor or stranger would come to our house in complain about him bullying others. I remember one day I was listening in Radio Bombo and there was News about him, I heard his name (Boklit and Ely) and a different surname, but the address of the suspect is our house. We heard the blotter about him, it was reported that he hit one of the guy with the tennis racket. The victim was the son of a very influential person in the province.

Boklit my brother said; "I hated him, I actually asked him to have a fist fight with me but because he was so big so I let him go first and then while he was walking ahead of me, I was behind him and I hit him with a tennis racket at the back. It was pre-meditated though." So when we heard it on Bombo radio, we were just laughing not for what he did and for the bad things he did but because we heard his name "Boklit" but his last name was different. (Our uncle had different reporting, he got it right). So we were just laughing at him. He made up the name and when he went to Manila and then to America, I realized that. I realize that he was very smart because he gave them the wrong name that's why he did not have the police record.

I also remember when my mother send him to my brother in Paglaum Sports Complex so he could be with him and so he (my big brother) could go to watch over him. I remember when he became the Caretaker at the Paglaum Tennis Club at the Northern side, and I was at the Southern side working as a ball boy and, at the same time, we go to school. I was the one who does the laundry of pastor Ely, but, sometimes, he don't pay me anything. He doesn't give me anything, and, sometimes, he'd promised me to give me money for doing his laundry, but nothing, nothing.

I remember when he had problem at the said club that he went back home. He went home, but my dad kicked him out because of his notorious actions. Boklit's life was bad. He was very notorious that he left for Manila, thinking he can just escape life just like that.

Nevertheless, I got his address, so I started to send him some letters and put some gospel tracks in the mailing envelope. I remember when I graduated high school he asked me what I want for a gift, and I told him I wanted a dictionary; then, he sent me a large print dictionary from Manila, and that's what I used when I was in college. That dictionary was the only gift that I really treasure from him. I really wanted for him to come back to God, and I wanted for him to return to God. All I know that he was doing a lot of bad things inside that night club. I cannot mention it, but I believe he was involved in so many bad things, and I know he was working there as a waiter or DJ (Disc Jockey). When we were talking about his job as a DJ, he sent me a cassette tape that has no gap in it. It was all dance music or disco music or collection of disco music.

I was very happy when I heard that he went to Baguio city to my older brother. I was happy he was courageous enough when he quit his job and went to Baguio city to my brother who is a pastor in that place.

We were informed by my brother that Boklit was in trouble, he was beat up to almost to death. My brother told us that there were about 10 people who beat him up when he was working in the night club. I believe I heard that that was the turning point of his (Boklit's) life.

One of the things that really made an impact in his life was also some of the letters and encouragement that I sent him including the tracks when he was still in a disco pub. There was no point that I did not remind him about the Lord Jesus Christ and His grace in my letter to Boklit, the gospel tracks that I really choose to send him. I have to spend the time and money so I could have or I could see him back to the Lord. When I heard that he came back and went to college in the seminary, I was so happy.

When I started my vocational school, he was the one who financially supported me. Unfortunately, I did not finish my degree on vocational course, and I end up in a seminary, but I was grateful he supported me during those times.

What I didn't like with Boklit was, he really was bully and he was greedy. If he did not like to share it, he would spit on his food. He always wanted to come home and he wanted to make sure that there is food on the table but he is not helping and providing for the needs at home. He was selfish and wouldn't share his money. Boklit was the black sheep among us, and he did not concentrate on his studies.

I remember that I always hear Boklit talked back to

our dad, and our mother was the only one who tried to protect him. He was drinking and smoking marijuana. I sometimes use him as an example to the children at school. I told them that I witnessed people who were hooked on those. Some of the children would ask me, is it you, sir? And I told them no, it's my siblings. I remember that when they smoke marijuana, I can smell the smoke from somewhere, so I know the smell of marijuana because of them who used it. Even if they were so far away from me, I tried to smell it to know it, so I know the smell of marijuana.

We were all been beaten up by our dad. Not so much of me. I felt so bad when I see my siblings being beat up by our dad. I know the pain that they we're going through because… If one of our siblings is being beat up by our dad, I know that I will be next.

I remember when Ely went to Guimaras Island to study. When my dad took him there, I know what is in his mind, it's hard. He went to IloIlo in Good Shepherd Fold Academy until he made the pastor there very disappointed of him for all the bad things he did there in that academy.

My name is Samson and known as Sammy to my friends. I'm a family man, a pastor and an evangelist. About my dad's attitude towards me, he was always mad at me. My anger of him was still there because he did not like us to be pastors because he only wanted Ephraim to be the pastor in the family. When he came to know the Lord, it was the only time that I pulled up all my anger to him and made him see that I was really was that bad. I don't know if Ely showed his anger to our dad when he became a Christian. I don't know if Ely really showed his anger of any sort, but, for me, every time my dad sees me, I really wanted to show to him that I'm doing stupid things such as smoking. I really wanted for him to see me drinking wine, and he would yell at me that's enough. He would tell me that smoking and drinking are not good for me. I really poured out everything in front of him.

I know that Ely went through a lot of ups and downs in his life before he came to know the Lord and before he became a pastor. I know that it hurts me to just think of all the beatings that he went through under my dad's hands. He went- I know he went through a lot in the hands of my dad with all that pain that our dad did to him. I know our dad is already dead. But, it was hard. Our mother is the one who defended us inside the house whenever we have problems with our dad.

For me, I can tell what our dad will do to Ely. But Ely was determined to be a pastor after he came to know the Lord. It was that time that the pride of our dad was there, and that he was proud that his children are rebellious and a problem in the community instead of becoming pastors. It was hard for him... if he accepted all his faults and his bad treatment to us. Although I already have my own family, I will tell my mother about our problems during those times, and she would tell me what to do and let me sleep in her lap. Just like when we were little, she would let us sleep in her lap or chest. She was very sweet, very loving, and caring. Our mother is very beautiful. She has a Spanish heritage.

Every time we were in trouble with our dad, many times our mother was the one who got hit in the body by the beatings of our dad to us. If that happens, that's the only time that our dad would stop. I don't know if Ely's head has been put and tied inside the antique jar we called banga. Sometimes, he would banged our heads or put our head inside the head of the jar. Our mother would always stand in between of us when dad was violent and in raged or when he beat us up. Sometimes, when our cousins- the sisters of our mom, would hear a commotion in our house, when my dad was beating us up, they would come out of their house and would tell our dad to stop. And that's the only time our dad will stop.

People during those times, especially our aunties and uncles would come out of their house and plead to our dad for us, and in our behalf. Because even if we would run away from our house trying to escape the violence and the beatings, my dad would still run after us on the alley outside.

Our dad would hit us with the piece of wood or with belt. I remember one day our dad came home with the tail of a ray fish for us. I don't know if Ely was been hit by the tail of the ray fish, but it really hurts. I remember our grandmother was so mad at my dad because he used the tail of the ray fish to hit us. Sometimes, my heart breaks, and it hurts to go through the pain that you don't understand.

I was thinking of our siblings and our brother Rosendo who did not even say good bye to him and tell him of his plan to become a pastor. I used to say if there is no God and our older brother Rosendo did not become a pastor in our life, our home would have been all criminals. That's why I understand all those who were doing bad things in life because of what they saw inside their house. It's where it started; that's where it started. That's why when I had my own family; I promised that I'm not going to do something violent to them. I always give warning to my children before about 3 to 4 warnings and if they continue doing such… and everyday they keep on doing it, I punch them and that's it. I have a son who is now a pastor, and when I told him once not to go to such places and he went, I beat him up and told him it's because I don't want or I don't like the place that he went into. The next morning, he talked to me, and he was already 3rd year in electrical engineering, and he told me he's going to quit school. I asked him his plans. He said, "I wanted to be a pastor." I told him, it's up to him. He said to me, "Are you going to support me?" Of course it's a yes, but I still have to figure it up.

I do evangelism at daytime and at night I was drunk. I do evangelism on daytime, but there I was drunk at night because I wanted to show it to my dad that I was rebellious. But it was different what I did to my son who went to the place that I don't want him to go although I beat him up, but still he became a pastor.

Our mother and father were Catholics and our grandmother was Catholic, even having imported religious images she got from Spain and Portugal. There are some images that she got from the river that were coming from the hospital. We picked up junk and bottles, all kinds of metals and fire woods from that river where all those things were coming from the hospital. That's where we got some of the images that my grandmother worshipped. We are so glad our grandmother and parents came to know the Lord late in their lives.

There are a lot of people around us and those who brought in some cults doctrines and practices in our house. We have neighbors who were bringing in evil spirits. We had neighbors who lived downstairs and we saw some evil spirits in that neighbor's house and they were helping them (my mother and grandmother) do such. They practice divination cults and the necromancy and other evil spirit practices that are purely evil.

When my dad became a Christian, he would tell me you smell like cigarettes or you smell liquor or wine. Sometimes, when I go to church, I would smoke outside first before getting in, and I would drink and then I'll get in to the church and sit next to my dad and he would tell me you come in to the church and you smell cigarettes and liquor. My oldest brother who is a pastor was the one who told him about the Lord, about salvation. He was angry and, sometimes, he would curse our brother. We kept on testifying to him until he came to know the Lord and became a changed man.

Then, Ely got saved and has been doing all the good things to my father and soon after, forgave him. But for me, oh, every time I go to church, I would make sure and show him that I was rebellious or bad. I remember when my dad was dying and in his deathbed, my sister called me, but I did not hear her and my mom said that my dad was calling me. They said my dad wanted to say something to me, but I already left because I told my dad that I was going to Silay City to witness to his relatives. Just by the time I left, my dad passed away.

Ely was in America and my dad can't talk, and he was just whispering the words. They said he was asking for forgiveness, and he also was actually asking for Ely's forgiveness to him.

During those times, I would always pass by my dad's side or in front of him making him smell my breath, and he would always say you smell bad, you smell wine or smoke. When my dad came to know the Lord in 1982, it was almost the same year that Ely came to know the Lord Jesus Christ. That's why when he became a Christian, I want for him to feel what I felt and he would tell me to wash or brush my teeth, and I was thinking I thought this is what he likes before, and now, he hated it.

When he was an unbeliever and when I come to a party in our relative's house, he would always tell me Samson is here give him some glass and make him drink.

I want to win souls for Christ and preach to his cousins and relatives. I want to tell them that my dad became a changed man. During those times, I really had a bad feeling with my dad when he was in his deathbed. I told him what was in my heart. Although I was already a pastor, I still have some bitterness on my dad that's why a week before he died, I told him frankly what was in my heart and why I was doing all the bad things I was doing. What I was doing was the things he used to do because I want for him to feel what I felt.

Although at that time, I was not in full-time ministry. However, three months before he passed away, I became a full-time minister. Before he died at around 8 o'clock in the morning, I did not know that he died already because like I said to him, I'm going to Silay City, and I'm going to his relatives to tell them about him and about the God who changed him. When I came home, my mom told me that my dad was calling me, but I didn't hear him when I left.

Director Vic Tiro was asking Samson how he coped up with his bitterness on our dad. Samson said, "One week before he died, I told him that I'm preaching, I belong to God, and I wanted to reach out to all your loved ones; I want them to know Him or lead them to the feet of God." Samson forgave his dad and was present all the time during his dad's funeral.

My real name is Remigio (aka Nene). Our life before was really hard. One time in my life, I also went to Manila to try to adventure. Ely went to Manila because there is no future in our place. The salary of our father is not enough to support us. Our dad was an alcoholic and was always in a nearby cockpit arena. I'm the 5th of all living siblings. Our dad use to work at the provincial Capitol. He was a carpenter, but that was not a stable job. Sometimes, in just after a month, he'll lose his job as a carpenter. That's why we became ball boys at the tennis court. We got up at 5:00 in the morning to start working as ball boys at the tennis court. We do that so we could have money when we go to school because we sometimes don't have breakfast at home. It was not always clear if we will have food on the table in the morning, so we have to do ball boy at the tennis court to earn 10 cents. Only then we are sure to have money for school and for lunch. That's a lot of money already during the seventies. As we reached high school, life began to be more difficult for all of us.

I became a tennis trainer that's why I always have money in my pocket during my high school days. I study, but, sometimes, I have to miss classes at least once or twice a week so I could have money. We didn't do a full week of school for lack of money for transportation. Every school day, we are hesitant to go because we don't know if we'll have breakfast or even coffee, and, then, when we come back home, we don't know if we have food on the table, and if we do, we might have just have rice and that's it. We only have rice for lunch and nothing else.

I left my work as a ball boy and became a tennis trainer. The only siblings that did not worked hard like us who worked as a ball boy in Negros Occidental Tennis Association (NOTA) was our brother Ephraim; he did not work there in NOTA as a ball boy. I believe it's one of the reasons why Ely forced himself to go to Manila to work in a night club. I believe it was a gay bar. I don't know. Then, after sometimes, he went to our brother who is a pastor in Baguio City.

Our mother can't do anything because our dad didn't care about us. Our mom will do the same; she will sit with us or on the side, and suffer hunger with us. We were very poor. We did not have electricity, we did not have running water and we have to make a way to feed ourselves because there's nothing that we can do but to work so we can eat. I was already a trainer at the tennis court and I earned five pesos. Back then, five pesos was a lot of money already. Ely he sings in a Folk house when he was a young man. He sang the songs of John Denver, Beatles, Peter Paul and Mary, Basil Valdez and other Balladeer and Folk Singers' songs. But me, I don't have any plans and wherever I go and on whatever I do, that's what I do. Some of my siblings, they became members here in evangelical church.

I was better off than them when we were young because sometimes I would be the one who would share for the needs at home. I have money, not so much but we get to get better off a little bit because of what I earned. I was next to Samson but Ely was a tough guy, he is respected by the people his age and some older people here. Our buddies, they don't make fun of him; they were scared of him, and he was respected here. People and our friends made fun of me, but they don't do that to Ely; they are scared of him. Ely is just quiet, but, sometimes, he's dangerous. He always had a fight with my dad and we were the one who tried to stop him, and we were the one who tried to mediate and calm them down. Ely would sometimes just blow off especially when he's drunk and start the fight and he would argue with everyone. There are times he will swear at us. We don't want to stay at home because we don't want to be beat up or swear, cursed or scolded by our dad.

We were a broken family. When we come home late at night, my father would locked the door already, and we have to go through under the floor so we can get in inside the house because we were scared of being caught by him in the middle of the night. Or worse, be beaten up. We don't have a good bed and our table is very small. When we sleep, we just pile up in one place

Our youngest brother, Pastor Gideon, also had a fight with our dad. We remember him telling us that he threatened our dad, and he told dad that he can fight back already because our dad is too old to have a fist fight with him. He did it before he went to Manila, and during those times, he was still single.

I remember my dad would tell us that if we get caught skipping school, he will beat us up, and I told him I'm not asking anything from him. I told him, "I don't ask anything from you. I went to school, and I never ask money from you." He never paid for my uniform fees and other expenses; it's all on us and we don't have to ask anything from him. Its better now, we're bit better off now because of what happened to us. We don't want our own children to go through with what we've been to. I told my children to study hard. Before, I'm just a tennis trainer and coach. However, I tried to make a way that when I come to know someone who is a manager of a sugar-milling company we called Central, I asked him for a stable job. You see, we tried to make some ways.

I smoked marijuana when Mike was my best friend, and, during those times, marijuana was just a Peso and 50 cents per matchbox. That was on the seventies, so it was cheap. There was a time that dad hit me with ray fish tail, and it really hurts. I experienced it because I was out of the house at night during that time. Our dad comes home late at night drunk to cause trouble in our house. If our dad attitude and beatings at us happens today in terms of what he was doing to us, he could have been in jail already for all the abuses that he did to all of us… But our dad became a changed man. He started working in the church. My dad went to Manila, Mandaluyong, and Malabon during Ely's wedding with Vemerlyn and those were the days when he was still very strong.

He was a good man and a faithful servant of God; he was really different, and he was really faithful. I was told by Reverend Noly Bustamante what he said about our dad, he said; "I'd never seen such a faithful man of God such as your dad. Is he one of the pastors at the church?" Our dad, after he became a born again believer, he was at church every day, but before he came to know the Lord Jesus Christ, he swear and cursed too much, but his encounter with the Lord changed him.

Since he became a believer, he would tell me that I don't want to get married because I just want to come home late at night drunk. He told me to get married already, so I don't have to come home late. Because during those times; when he already was a believer, I was at night club almost every night. The reasons why I was in a night club every night because I was making good money as a trainer. When I got married, Ely was already in Manila.

There was really a big change in my dad's life. He was trusted by the church of the money, which he will also deposit to the bank. My dad has been robbed several times because of that.

I also remember that I saw Ely on television at Monico Puentebella's program "Monico" and on Saturday Special and other TV programs. I didn't really see much of what was happening during those times because I didn't stay at home those times, I was at Olongapo City or somewhere else. I was a professional tennis player, and I played in tournaments, Professional Games and Palarong Pambansa (National Competition). I won a lot of trophies and gold medals in tennis. I used tennis as my stepping stone to get a good job, a good paying job. Our dad died of sickness in 2002, but our mom died of vehicular accident.

My name is Eduardo Rodriguez and my nickname is "Potot," which means "shorty." We used to live just next to Negros

Occidental Tennis Association (NOTA). At the moment of this interview, I'm already 56 years old. We are 6 in the family, and there were only 3 of us who went to school. While we were going for school, we have to work at the tennis court as a ball boy. Right now, we are still here in the Bacolod City. Just like I said, before we go to school, we have to work as a ball boy so we could have money at school because our parents cannot afford to support us. When I grew up, I started to play tennis, and I started to also work as a trainer at the tennis court so I could finish my schooling in high school. Pastor Ely is my 2nd cousin; he also played tennis, and we used to live in the same house. They lived downstairs, and we were up stairs. One day, there was a Bible study in our neighbor, and we were invited to attend. It was there that I came to know the Lord Jesus Christ in that Bible study.

I remember those days when we were being teased and called as pastors. We felt like we were being persecuted. I remember it was 1975, and I was in 2nd year high school. I was enrolled in the different high school, and, eventually, I joined my siblings on the other school where they were in enrolled so we could be together. Then, I remembered I started moving away from the truth. I know that my moved from church was off and was a dead moved. But I continued my studies and, unfortunately, my parents will just visit us during special occasions and graduations. The sad thing is that my parents don't support us financially. The three of us, we went to school until we finish our high school. I really wanted to go to college, but we cannot afford to send ourselves, so we decided to just stop schooling.

Pastor Ely is a joker, that's one of the things that I cannot forget about him. Pastor Ely is really pleasant to be with. When we were together, we all have fun and makes jokes. In everything that we do, we always have fun. I remember watching a movie with pastor Ely about Dolphy, so it was a comedy. It was so funny and everyone of course was laughing and we cannot hear the audio in the theater or the movie because it was so loud, and when everyone stopped laughing, pastor Ely started laughing so loud alone, by himself... So when all the people in the theater heard him laugh so loud, they all laughed again. Everyone was wondering why he was laughing by himself when the scene was not funny at all. Back in our younger days, we also pick fights against each other. We also did shine shoes together. We sell newspapers and sweepstakes in Bacolod Plaza.

I was just so surprised when I heard the news that he left for Manila and also I heard the news that he became a pastor and went to America. Although I still have some friends here, Pastor Ely is my only best friend here. Those are the things that I cannot forget about my friend; I must really confess. Pastor Ely when he was here long time ago, he was very violent. Despite that, I don't hear him taking drugs because he never showed it to me when we were together. I was only 19 years old when I married my wife who was then 18 at the time. Pastor Ely was one of the sponsors on my son's dedication. He is my best friend.

What Boklit's Old Time Friends Says About Him

"I used to do outreach classes at your residence near the tennis court. One of the many things that stand-out in my mind about you is you're being a joker. It was Bacolod Baptist Church Youth Camp at Ma-ao. We pitched a tent outside the residence of the Padilla's family. About 15 campers stayed in that tent of around 4x4 meters. I remember you shaved off your hair; I didn't know why. It's was never a style or new-fashioned to have skin head or being bald as a youth. At the camp, the young people can't stop laughing and called you "Mr. Clean" referring to the bald giant in the laundry soap ad on TV and promos. I got mad because it was way past bedtime and everyone kept laughing because you were making jokes. Every time I called and yelled at to everyone to keep quiet, the campers just answered me, "It's because Mr. Clean is funny." They were referring to Ely. But secretly, I was laughing myself. God bless your ministry, Ely." Elvie Jamelo

"I remember that Ely R. Sagansay… besides the fact that I always see you in all church activities and Youth Camps, I remember you being so diligent in church's chores, and you always wear jean pants and at times without a shirt. You do the laundry and help with the carpentry, and running errands. We went together in many outreach programs and Bible studies. You were always there making jokes and having fun. Ely, I remember you being with Benjie Padrones, too. I've observed and seen how God have been so faithful to you because of your faithfulness to Him in the ministry and in the church. God bless you and your ministry, Pastor Ely." -Bing Joy Togle

More of What Others Say About the Author

My name is Ismael 'Mait' Lizardo, pastor Ely's cousin. When we were young, we lived in the troubled place in Bacolod City Negros Occidental. That was when we were not Christians yet. Our lives were messed up. We were buddies; there were four in the group, and we were cousins. It was Boklit, Potot, Popoy, and my self- (Mait). We were always at the tennis court. We played tennis, and, sometimes, we trained people play tennis. At times, we worked as ball boys. That was our job; we started as ball boys at the tennis court and then we became tennis trainers. During our times, we would go out from the tennis court to hang out and play. In few times, we would be bystanders until we start some trouble to other kids from the other blocks of our village. And there, we always have the fight with other kids, and we would throw stones at them. Our place was filled with troubles. Some of our buddies would run away and try to get away from us. We want to get out, but we could not get out of trouble. It's always there. We were stuck in what we do as kids because that was the only thing we can do at the tennis court. Nevertheless, we would play and sing songs at the street corner. I remember

Ely can sing really good, such as the songs of John Denver and John Lennon, so he'd always lead the drinking and singing session.

Once in a while, we would get out of the tennis court looking for some other job because we don't always make good money at the tennis court. We sell newspapers. We will start from Lopez Jaena to Bacolod plaza, and occasionally in front of Sea Breeze hotel. Boklit was very diligent because he really tried to sell more newspapers. I remember that day he tried to go across Sea Breeze hotel but he was hit by a car. I know it was a De luxe kind of car. I was scared. My eyes saw the accident. We were glad he was all right and he survived. I didn't know he was really hurt when he was taken to the hospital. Praise the Lord he was well after that incident.

I remember that Boklit followed his dream and went to Manila. I know his love story. He used to have a beautiful girlfriend we called in our dialect 'morena'. It means she has a fine, smooth, and light brown skin. At that time, Boklit was willing and so ready to marry her, but, unfortunately, his girlfriend went to Manila. I remember that time when Boklit tried his way to go to Manila. After those times, I lost communication with him. A few years later, I went to Manila, and I never saw him since until I heard the news from Bacolod that he started to work at the disco house. I know that he will make it there as a DJ because he is very good at music. However, he was a big time mess, and it's like those were the worst moment in his life. He even has a death threat. I heard that some people that he did not know were looking for him ready to kill him. He shared it to me that someone in the club pointed a gun on his head, a 45 caliber on him in the night club where he was working.

Boklit started looking for me here in Malabon. I was surprised when he showed up at my door. I was a faithful member of the local church there during those days and I know that he was in these worldly things. I remember Boklit brought with him a small Bible. I was surprised to see him read the Bible. When he came to my place, he asked me if he could stay in my place because he said he didn't want to stay in his job anymore.

I remember that he always carry a small Bible in his pocket. I was surprised when he told me this one day: "Brother Ismael, I wanted to attend a church." But I told him that I am already a member of the Iglesia ni Cristo (Church of Christ) so he asked me if there's a church that he can attend here in Malabon, so I told him of a place I attended during Easter Service few years back. When we get there, I was surprised that the church was already big with whom Dr. Pio S. Tica is the pastor. To make the long story short, we became members of International Baptist Church in Malabon. At first, I told Boklit to just keep on going there. I said to him; "Boklit, you can just go there because you see I'm already in Iglesia ni Cristo. So I still am not ready, I am already a church member." So, he told me to come with him to the church and then he'll come to my church. After Boklit surrendered his life to God, he enrolled in a Bible college at the seminary founded by Dr. Gavino S. Tica.

Boklit became a pastor of Asiel Baptist Church-Makati as he continued to study in a Bible college. I believe he became a pastor there in just a few years. Then,

I lost communication with him again. From what I know, Boklit remained faithful to God, and I can say that he really is a changed man.

I remember Boklit joined the singing competition and, also, he was guesting on television show. I witnessed all those accomplishments, but I believe that he is using it now for his ministry and for the Lord. Today, I had seen those dreams from his children, too.

I remember when we were little kids we gamble, and we were bad and rebellious to our parents. I believe that God took us to Manila so we could be the light in the dead city through God's Word.

Boklit's dad is a great testimony to me, too, and to others. Boklit's parents brought my family to the Lord. I believe they were the one who led my mom to the Lord. Our parents were dead; they all passed away, but I know that they came to know the Lord because of Boklit's parents.

To Boklit, I always remember seeing you always praying and reading your Bible with tears in your eyes. I can still picture in my mind seeing the skinny you with a long hair like an ex- convict. But now the Lord gave you a good life. You are blessed pastor, Ely.

Words from Reverend Dean Mileto- The life of Pastor Ely Roque Sagansay is a story of victory. Up against insurmountable odds, this man, by the grace of God overcame the grimmest of circumstances.

One of my first recollections of Pastor Ely was when our church took up an impromptu offering for his short-term Mission Trip to the Philippines. I was overwhelmed and amazed at the response of the people of Gilead Baptist Church of Taylor as they kept coming forward and placing their money in a large basket for Ely's trip. This "processional" lasted for few minutes at the closing of our worship. However, as the offering was unfolding; I watched Ely of which at that time I don't really know much about him, but watching him on the platform was gripping. As he stood with our Senior Pastor Tom Downs, I watched him cry as he shared his mission minded heart in front of the congregation, which brought many to tears as they gave that day. Since that time, what I know about Ely Sagansay and his wife Vemerlyn is that they are "the real deal".

I heard someone defined character as- "Character is who you are when no one else is around." I can tell you this, that when they are serving away from the crowd, I have witnessed dedication, humility, and a God-driven desire to serve others. Many times, I've witnessed the hours of work, and their own resources dedicated to the service of the King and the people of the Philippines.

As you read Boklit, you find a story of this man who was raised in not only poverty, but abject poverty. What's the difference? Abject poverty is defined as "a condition characterized by severe deprivation of basic human needs, including food, safe drinking water, sanitation facilities, health, shelter, education and information." This is the humble beginnings for young Ely Sagansay. But if that wasn't bad enough, he goes on to describe his daily encounters with his father which can only be described as violent and menacing. However, given these grave beginnings, the story of Boklit has an ending that can only be described as "Amazing Grace". Our God is good and His grace is revealed in the life story of "Boklit". - Reverend Dean V. Mileto

Luth Jardinel's Brief Interview with Pastor Ely

Luth: You've not talked much about your academics in this narrative, so we know a little of your writing pursuits. When did you first realize you wanted to write?

Ely: Since I was in high school, I can tell already that I can write especially when I was in the seminary because I like essay-type tests. English and Speech was my favorite subjects, and I always get the highest grades in them. I did not finish high school. I flunked for lacked of attendance. When I write my first sermon then until now, it was always in English. Despite that, I never thought of being an author. It's a very long story why I became an Author.

Luth: Since you already mention your seminary days, how different was it from the past schools you've attended? I'm coming from the idea that you flunked in high school yet successfully graduated in a seminary.

Ely: It was lacked of attendance at high school, and I was serious in my studies during my seminary days because I've realized that I can't make it in life by just singing or working in a club.

Luth: What was the best memory you have of your father?

Ely: When I came home from Manila. He picked me up from the pier and gave me a hug and a kiss for the first time.

Luth: What happened to the girl you followed in Manila? How did you part ways?

Ely: Her parents, uncle and cousins were not in favored of me because of my lifestyle, and they think I was not the man for her. Her uncle is well off in Makati and probably her parents because she used expensive clothes. She started not seeing me and she just disappeared in our relationship. She may have went back to Bacolod City.

Luth: If you were talking to Boklit now, what would you tell him?

Ely: I'm going to ask him these questions: "If the Lord will let you start all over again like from nothing, and ask you what kind of life do you want and the parents you choose to grow up with, whose life would that be and which parents?"

Luth: As a person who was once "Boklit," what would you like to tell Boklits of today?

Ely: Be different, follow your dreams, and don't be afraid to fail. You love more, serve more, and put God first in your life. Have a relationship with God and maintain a good relationship with family, friends and others. Salvation of man's soul... Get an Education and pick what you love to learn about and really wanted to work for as long as you live. Be sure to pick the right person to marry. It's Salvation, Education, and your Decision to a lifetime relationship- your future spouse. If you succeed in life; be humble and stay humble. Don't be afraid to take some risks and be weird with your dreams and vision in life. Be yourself. Live with integrity, dignity and transparency. Love God and love your family. I hope I make sense and if I don't, the next Boklit must have...

About the Author

Reverend Ely Roque Sagansay was born in Bacolod City, Philippines. He is a graduate of International Baptist Theological College in Mandaluyong, Metro Manila, Philippines. Ely was once a classroom teacher. For five years, he was a radio host of the program Gideon 300 at DWGO AM Radio based in Olongapo City, Philippines. Ely also started the radio program "Love is the Reason" used to air on Light House Radio 106.3 FM.

Ely was a professor and an administrator of the International Baptist Theological College extension school in Subic, Zambales. Still in the 90s, he served as the director of music at the Greater Detroit Baptist Association of the Southern Baptist Convention (SBC). A decade ago, he pioneered International Community Christian Church in Trenton, Michigan- (SBC). Ely has been a pastor for more than three decades.

Ely's life story was featured on Philippine television at 700 Club, a production show in GMA 7. It is available on You Tube at 700 Club Asia with the running title "Walwal": The Ely Sagansay Story.

Ely is the author of "Christmas Every Day," "Mi Daily Devotion" (First and Second Edition), and "Thanksgiving

Every Day" published by Westbow Press. He used to be a guest writer for News Herald- Downriver, Michigan in their Opinion section. He is the man behind the digital devotion site at www.boklitbook.com.

Based in Michigan, USA, Ely is married to Vemerlyn Dumala-Sagansay, now blessed by the Lord with four (4) children, namely: Eliezer, Ely Jr., Eliel Lyn, and Elmer John. All of them are God-fearing children and loves the Lord.

Special Thanks

Luth Lucero-Editor
Reverend Sammy "Samson" Sagansay
Reverend Ephraim "Gamay" Sagansay
Remigio "Nene" Sagansay
Aidariza "Deding" Sagansay
Mr. Eduardo "Potot" Rodriguez
Mr. Ismael "Mait" Lizardo
Mr. Ryan Drew Hoffman
Mrs. Elvie Jamelo
Mrs. Bing Joy Togle
Mr. Serlito Tiolo
Mr. Vic De La Cruz Tiro
Reverend Dean V. Mileto
Reverend Thomas 'Tom' Downs
DSWD (Social Marketing Service) - Philippines
Director Mr. Cezario Joel C. Espejo
Department of Social Welfare and
Development (DSWD) Philippines
Photographer: Elmer John "EJ" Dumala Sagansay

Ephel Sagansay
Special thanks to my dear wife Vemerlyn
Dumala Sagansay for her love and undying
support to me and my ministry

Endorsement

The life of Pastor Ely Sagansay is a story of victory. Up against insurmountable odds, this man, by the grace of God overcame the grimmest of circumstances.

As you read Boklit, you will find the story of a man who was raised in not only poverty, but abject poverty. What's the difference? Abject poverty is defined as "a condition characterized by severe deprivation of basic human needs; including food, safe drinking water, sanitation facilities, health, shelter, education and information." This is the humble beginnings for young Ely Roque Sagansay. But if that wasn't bad enough, he goes on to describe his daily encounters with his father which can only be described as violent and menacing. However, given these grave beginnings, the story of Boklit has an ending that can only be described as "Amazing Grace". Our God is good and His grace is revealed in the life story of "Boklit".

Reverend Dean V. Mileto
Staff Pastor- Gilead Baptist Church
Victory Bible Class
Director of Staff Development in Detroit, Michigan
Free Lance Consultant

East Detroit Schools and Huron Valley Schools, Michigan

Bachelor of Religious Education (BRE)

If there is a 'rewind' in this life; I would love to play the same role, with the same parents and siblings. I don't mind going through the same circumstances. I will choose the same wife, the same children, and the same ending as of the moment since we don't know what's ahead of us. But always be positive, hopeful and looking unto Jesus. Ely Roque Sagansay

Printed in the United States
By Bookmasters